Education and Social Justice

Education and Social Justice

Denis Lawton

University of London Institute of Education

SAGE Studies in Social and Educational Change
Volume 7

 SAGE Publications · London and Beverly Hills

For information address

SAGE Publications Ltd
28 Banner Street
London EC1Y 8QE

SAGE Publications Inc
275 South Beverly Drive
Beverly Hills, California 90212

International Standard Book Number
0 8039 9946 1 Cloth
0 8039 9867 8 Paper

Library of Congress Catalog Card Number
74-31568

First Printing

Printed in Great Britain by
Biddles Ltd, Guildford, Surrey

CONTENTS

INTRODUCTION

There are two major themes in the recent development of English education: the first is a drive to improve education for reasons of economic efficiency; the second is to achieve a greater degree of social justice in education, and by means of education. There is no essential conflict between these two major themes, but the emphasis changes from time to time. It might be an over-simplification to suggest that at times of optimism social justice prevails and that at times of insecurity, economic and otherwise, the efficiency argument tends to prevail. To explore that idea, however, is not the purpose of this book. The purpose is to concentrate on one of those themes — social justice — and to examine the reasons for the very slow rate of progress towards this goal.

In 1976 the British Prime Minister, James Callaghan, called for a great debate on education. He seemed to be particularly concerned about the relationship between education and economic efficiency. During 1976 there were also other moves in the direction of efficiency, sometimes in the name of standards, sometimes for reasons of public accountability, and sometimes as a reaction to revealed scandals in the educational system such as the collapse of the William Tyndale Primary School. We should certainly welcome the idea of a great debate but make sure that education does not

1

sacrifice the case for social justice in the name of greater economic efficiency. In his speech at Ruskin College in October 1976, the Prime Minister said that 'The goals of our education, from nursery school through to adult education, are clear enough. They are to equip children to the best of their ability for a lively constructive place in society and also to fit them to do a job of work. Not one or the other, but both.' He went on to suggest that whereas in the bad old days the emphasis had been on fitting people for work, in recent years the swing had been in the opposite direction. What the Prime Minister did not mention was that there has been very little progress in recent years towards the goal of a greater degree of social justice in education. If we are talking about the limited success of the educational system, we should put that up for consideration as well as the alleged failure of schools to equip children with the basic skills which would enable them to get useful jobs. There may indeed be connections between the two problems. I am going to suggest in this book that one reason for the limited success of schools is that educationists, including teachers, are too easily led astray by false theories. If we are to achieve greater social justice in education, and greater efficiency, we must clarify the purpose of education in a democracy and demonstrate what is wrong with certain fashionable theories or pseudo-theories.

I suggest that the study of the curriculum is crucial to any discussion of this kind, but in the past it has been almost totally ignored. I will conclude the book by outlining a theory of curriculum planning which might go some way towards clarifying the issues as well as making possible a more enlightened policy in educational matters. I am suggesting, therefore, that the goals are *not* yet clear enough — especially in terms of the content of the curriculum — and that the pathway to clarification is obscured by bad theories.

1

SOCIAL JUSTICE
AND EDUCATION

The 1944 Education Act was in many respects a landmark. It
established secondary education as a legal right for all
children. Yet in some ways progress in secondary education
since then has been extremely disappointing. The rate of
truancy is high, many schools provide what could only be
described as an inferior education, and much less progress has
been achieved regarding equalizing educational opportunities
in secondary schools. The problem that Brian Simon
described in 1965 has by no means disappeared:

> It is now clear that the main inequalities in British education today
> are due to three factors: differences in social class, in sex, and
> geographical location . . .
> The Cardiganshire middle-class boy has roughly 160 times as much
> chance of reaching full-time higher education than the West Ham
> working-class girl; and this when the country has, in a formal sense,
> committed itself to a policy of equality of opportunity.
>
> (Address given at the Annual Conference of the Confederation for
> the Advancement of State Education, 1965, reprinted in Simon,
> 1971: 166.)

In this book I want to concentrate on one of the major

3

factors, namely differences in social class, and to suggest that the problem is much wider than access to certain kinds of educational institutions such as university, but that within secondary schools there is a general failure to make any significant step towards greater social justice in education. Of course there have been some improvements — the move towards abolishing segregation of children by means of types of schools and devices such as streaming — but for the majority of children schools still fail to provide basic educational rights and anything like equality of access to worthwhile knowledge and experiences.

Most schools have failed in this respect. Why?

It is too easy to blame this general failure (admitting the existence of many good and 'successful' schools) on a lack of financial resources. Of course many schools would do better with more money, and better resources. Of course there are schools like London's Thomas Calton School which are prevented from making advances by buildings which are scandalously inadequate. But this is too obvious an explanation and it is, in my view, by no means a totally convincing explanation. There are some schools where money and resources have been poured in on a lavish scale and they have still failed. Why?

It is also too easy to blame the failure on the teachers. Of course, the teaching profession is generally conservative, and of course there are some lazy and inefficient teachers, but it is quite wrong to try to blame teachers for the fact that most schools fail a sizeable proportion of their pupils. The major explanation of educational failure is that educational policy-making since 1944 has been pathetically inadequate. The 1944 Education Act provided a framework for secondary education for all. The framework itself was incomplete and the terminology ambiguous, but it was a major step forward in declaring publicly that all children had a right to secondary education. The failure to provide secondary education in a meaningful form for many children is a failure of policy. But why is there no clear policy? I suggest that this is a complex problem: on the one hand the difficulty of providing an acceptable theory of education in a pluralistic society; on the other the survival of many false educational doctrines in popular consciousness long after they have been discredited academically or have ceased to be compatible with a democratic society.

So I would attribute blame partly to the continued influence of out-of-date reactionary ideas, and partly to those who consider themselves to be 'progressive' but who perpetuate false doctrines or misinterpret and distort educational theories in a way which reduces the possibility of improving educational opportunities.

Sound educational practice must be based on sound educational theory; the following five chapters will be concerned with five misleading or 'bad' theories. Two of them are right-wing doctrines — social and intellectual elitism — which have distorted so much work in comprehensive schools. Chapters 4, 5 and 6 are concerned with some of the errors of the left: Chapter 4 on the ideas of those who put forward an exaggerated child-centred 'progressive' kind of schooling; Chapter 5 on the 'relativists' who are especially confused about the content of education, and Chapter 6 on the deschoolers, who despair so much about schools that they would abolish them altogether. I have said that these last three views are associated with the political left; I am not sure how much meaning left and right still have in politics, but if there is still a meaningful left-wing position in education I would see it as advocating complete equality of access to worthwhile experiences. If this definition is accepted then the progressives, the relativists and the deschoolers should not be classified as left-wing but might be more appropriately considered as bourgeois romantics.

Before going on to examine these false doctrines, however, it may be useful to outline my position on social justice and education. It would clearly be a mistake to take for granted the validity of the idea of social justice in education: as Tawney pointed out as long ago as 1931 when discussing equality of opportunity:

> The conception is one to which homage is paid today by all, including those who resist most strenuously attempts to apply it. But the rhetorical tribute which it receives appears sometimes to be paid on the understanding that it shall be content with ceremonial honours, (Tawney, *Equality,* p. 103).

Ideas like equality, equality of opportunity, even secondary education for all mean different things to different people and different groups of people. It is also very easy for politicians to point in the direction of an idea like equality and at the same time cynically steer firmly away from it.

Partly for this reason I avoided using a term like 'equality in education' as a title for this book; partly also because it does beg a number of questions. It is quite possible to interpret 'equality' in such a way as to be against it, but I do not see how anyone pretending to support the idea of democracy, however defined, can be against the ideal of justice. That would be tantamount to supporting sin and opposing virtue. But it does make it necessary to say exactly what is meant by social justice in education: and this will also inevitably involve some attempts to clarify 'equality', 'equality of opportunity', 'secondary education for all' and even 'comprehensive education'. I am a little reluctant to embark on this kind of activity partly because this is a fairly well-trodden path. Tawney tried to clear up the confusion in the book I have already quoted; more recently Peters has dealt with the concept equality from a philosophical point of view in his *Ethics and Education.* Nevertheless, I think it will be necessary to state a position, even if it is a fairly obvious position, before going on in later chapters to criticize the views of others who are, in my view, partly responsible for the failure — or limited success — of schools in this respect.

One of the problems of using terms like equality and equality of opportunity in education is that they might be interpreted as meaning that everyone should have *exactly* the same education. This is clearly absurd, but not necessarily for the reasons which are sometimes suggested. Some of the objections to the idea of equality are extremely confused and Tawney dealt with them at some length. For example, he quoted (p. 44) Lord Birkenhead's declaration that the idea that men are equal is a 'poisonous doctrine'. A number of other people have also stated that equality is nonsense because human beings are simply not equal. Some men are taller than others; some men are more intelligent. But that is to miss the point, as Tawney pointed out:

> So to criticise inequality and to desire equality is not, as is some-
> times suggested, to cherish the romantic illusion that men are equal in
> character and intelligence. It is to hold that, while their natural
> endowments differ profoundly, it is the mark of a civilised society to
> aim at eliminating such inequalities as have their source, not in
> individual differences, but in its own organisation, and that in-
> dividual differences, which are a source of social energy, are more
> likely to ripen and find expression if social inequalities are, as far as
> practicable, diminished. (*Equality,* p. 57).

The point at issue then is not whether men are equal (clearly they are not, if equal means the same) but whether they should be treated equally — or to what extent they should be treated equally. The problem has been revived recently by

the whole question of sex equality. Men and women are not
the same but should they have the same kind of education?
Should they be treated equally? The legal answer now is that
they should and this is supported by powerful legal
machinery. But even the straightforward solution of treating
everyone equally is not easy to apply in education. Even in
such straightforward matters as distribution of food Peters
has pointed out that exceptions are made so that when we
have a system of food rationing, manual workers may get
slightly more food than office workers without there being
the feeling that this is unjust. This is related to Aristotle's
proposition that injustice may result from treating unequals
equally, as well as from treating equals unequally.

In education we have to ask whether a blind child or a
mental defective should have the same education as a normal
child or a highly intelligent child. To some extent this
problem has been solved since the Plowden Report by the
policy of *positive discrimination,* but as we shall see later on
this also begs a number of questions. One solution suggested
by Peters is that everyone *in a certain category* should be
treated equally. So within the category of mentally defective
all children ought to be treated the same as each other;
similarly all blind children should be treated with the kind of
positive discrimination which they have had for a number of
years. However, Peters himself points out that this can lead
to further difficulties. It may be possible for someone who
opposes the idea of equality but wishes to pay lip-service to it
to discover all sorts of differences between people which
might be used as grounds for treating people differently. We
might reject parents' income as irrelevant, but what about
intelligence? In recent years, especially since the development
of comprehensive schools, there has been an increased emphasis on the 'needs' of gifted children or exceptional
children who should be treated in some way differently from

the mass of the population. There is always the danger here of the ideal of fairness or social justice in terms of equality being accepted in principle but constantly finding that loopholes appear.

The case for treating people equally can be much strengthened by putting the principle in this way: 'No-one shall be presumed, in advance of particular cases being considered, to have a claim to better treatment than another'. (Peters, 1966: 121). Peters also points out that if the principle were stated in this way the onus would always be on the person wishing to treat people differently to justify that position. Other things being equal all people's claims should be equally considered. This of course does not solve the problem completely: it would be difficult to justify treating people differently in education on the grounds of parental income (despite the continued existence of public schools and other fee-paying schools in our society) but it might not be totally irrelevant to consider children with musical gifts as needing some kind of different educational treatment.

The whole difficulty in the field of education would appear to be that we have in the past been unclear about exactly *what* is being distributed when we are discussing the problem of distributive justice in the field of education. Peters (p. 123) points out that the notion basic to justice is that distinctions should be made if there are relevant differences and that they should not be made if there are no relevant differences or on the basis of irrelevant differences. But justice only operates in a situation which is in some ways 'rule governed': the point about justice is that it is the principle that there should be principles. It seems to me, and at this point I may be departing from Peters's argument, that the weakness of the argument for social justice in education, or equality in education, in the past, is that it has been stated in terms of equality of the right to *x* years of education or the right to enter a certain kind of educational institution, but what has not been done is to specify the kind of educational benefits to be made available in terms of *curriculum content*. It was therefore quite possible after the 1944 Education Act to satisfy certain kinds of argument about equality of opportunity in education by legislation for nine or ten years of compulsory education but then sending children at the age of 11 to such different kinds of institution that some schools were clearly inferior to others. In the same way it could now be argued that simply sending children to the same school does not guarantee equality of opportunity, if some children have *access to curriculum content* which is manifestly superior or inferior to what others are receiving. There is, of course, a difference here between stating the minimum requirements for an educated person in terms of curriculum content and saying that within any school every pupil has to have exactly the same curriculum. It is this kind of confusion in comprehensive schools which is bedevilling the whole issue of social justice in education at the moment. It seems to me that Peters (1966) was inconclusive about the question of equality in education, partly because he did not go on to stipulate what the educational content of compulsory schooling ought to be. I am not, of course, suggesting that the curriculum of schools should be restricted to a long list of behavioural objectives, starting at age 5 and finishing at age 16. What I am suggesting is that unless we define equality of educational opportunity in terms of the right to acquire certain kinds of knowledge and to be introduced to certain kinds of worthwhile experiences, then the idea of equality will remain hopelessly vague. Social justice in education is an empty slogan unless we are more precise about curriculum content.

I suggest therefore that we cannot get much farther along the road towards social justice in education in terms of treating people equally or unequally until we define some kind of legal minimum. We have already gone some way towards this — in a strange way — by making schooling compulsory until the age of 16 (even if parents do not want it!). Thus, children are guaranteed eleven years of schooling as a right. But this now seems to be putting the cart before the horse: surely it would have been better to have defined the kind of benefits to be attained by education before stipulating the number of years involved. A good deal of dissatisfaction by pupils and teachers alike has been generated by the fact that what children are meant to be doing in their eleven years (especially the last one or two) is far from clear. This suggestion is, of course, very different from saying that a curriculum should be stated in terms of specific lessons on specific days and so on as it has sometimes been suggested is the case in French schools. But if the state insists on children spending eleven years in school, this is an infringement of liberty, so it should also outline the benefits to be gained from schooling in terms of curriculum content.

This problem has been raised in a dramatic form by the recent legislation about sex discrimination in education. It is now illegal for a school to offer woodwork to boys, but to refuse it to the girls in the same schools. This produces a very strange situation: why should it be wrong for a girl in School A to be denied woodwork, if girls *and boys* in School B are always denied it because it does not appear in the curriculum? In other words it is futile to treat discrimination at a purely local or school level; if some aspects of the curriculum are really important, then a child in County Durham should have access to that kind of knowledge just as much as a child in Kent. In other words there is some need for a national statement about minimum curriculum requirements. Without this, discussion of sex discrimination or social justice in education is meaningless.

In essence what I am suggesting is this: to begin with the slogan of 'secondary education for all' was defined as a minimum number of years of schooling and the right of all children to have that period of time at a school. This was interpreted by most authorities as an invitation to run a segregated system of grammar schools and secondary modern schools. When it appeared that children going to these two different kinds of schools were being treated unequally to such an extent that some were regarded as successes and others as failures, then there was increased pressure to have common schools. However, it soon became apparent that even within comprehensive schools children receive different kinds of educational treatment, not all of which can be justified. There is now a need to talk about equality in terms of the content of education. Secondary education for all is meaningless, I suggest, unless we specify the benefits to be gained by education – that is, in the content of the curriculum. Equal opportunity in education would then mean equal access to worthwhile knowledge and experiences. This does not mean, however, that all children will have the same education. Having been exposed to the same kind of basic common core curriculum, there should always be opportunities available to allow children with special interests and abilities to pursue these interests and abilities to the highest possible level. What is not permissible in our society however is to give some children access to real education but to fob others off with sub-standard knowledge or experiences which are not worth while. To clarify this distinction it will be necessary to look more carefully at the whole process of selecting curriculum content and the justification of such selections. This is an aspect of educational theory and practice which has so far been badly neglected. I will come back to this problem in Chapter 8. Meanwhile I want to look at some of the theories, or non-theories, which have distracted educationists from what should have been a high priority in the years since 1944.

2

SOCIAL ELITISM

In Chapter 1 I suggested that one reason for educational failure in general, and in achieving social justice, was the lack of attention that had been paid to curriculum; I also suggested that this neglect of one aspect of educational theory was partly due to the survival or growth of bad theories of some kind. One of the theories which I want to examine I refer to as 'social elitism'. This is very much a hangover from the more rigid nineteenth-century social structure in which it was regarded as 'natural' for social classes to be treated differently in a whole range of respects including education. But I want to suggest that this kind of social elitism is still very much a part of popular thinking about education and a part of teacher thinking in particular. Sometimes there is an almost deliberate cloaking of privilege in terms of 'parental choice' or 'freedom of choice', but more importantly social elitism has survived as a part of the teacher-pupil relationship in which teachers think of certain kinds of children as automatically inferior or ineducable; and in particular this gives rise to teachers and educational decision-makers thinking that it is quite natural for one kind of child to have a different curriculum from another child from a different social group.

The assumption behind the false doctrine of social elitism is that breeding or rank or social class should determine the kind of education a person is given. This tradition has a long history and is still very much with us, either as an explicit justification for treating people differently in education (for example, Bantock), or as an implicit assumption that generalizations about education and social class are valid and should influence the treatment of individual children.

Let us look first of all at the development of the basic idea of breeding in the nineteenth century. It has often been pointed out that the origins of popular education in England were closely related to the prevailing nineteenth-century ideas on class. The early advocates of mass or popular education were careful to point out that the education they were proposing for the lower orders should not be confused with the kind of education recognized as appropriate for the upper and middle classes. One of the most interesting books on the history of elementary education in the nineteenth century is Mary Sturt's *The Education of the People* (1967). It is significant that the first chapter is called 'The importance of subordination'. The idea of keeping the lower orders in their place was partly a question of expediency: those in privileged positions of power, wealth and authority were anxious to hold on to the advantages bestowed upon them by their 'birth': 'If a horse knew as much as a man, I should not like to be his rider', said Mandeville when he opposed Charity Schools in 1723 (*Essay on Charity and Charity Schools*). But there were also many — probably a majority — who sincerely believed that high social rank carried with it a right to all sorts of privileges including a superior education. Such privileges were seen as 'natural' in a society which was only slowly changing from a hierarchical feudal system of ranks to stratification based on class. Even today the English class system is far from 'pure' — it still has vestiges of feudalism about it. We still have a House of Lords, partly based on the heredity principle, and to be a 'landed' country gentleman still carries high social status. This may well be connected with the fact that in England the social elitist view of education has survived longer than in the US or Western Europe.

Thus, when popular education developed in the first half of the nineteenth-century it was regarded as inevitable that there should be 'two nations' in education as in everything else:

> Working-class and middle-class education in the nineteenth century had clear identities. They were separated by different curricula, length of school life, attendance rates and cultural and social objectives.
>
> The continued existence of 'two nations' in education reflected a basic social reality. Commentators at mid-century were pointing not only to England's unprecedented industrial advance, but also to its disparate social effects. In the previous quarter of a century, said one writer in 1845, Britain in its industrialization had 'exhibited the most extraordinary spectacle that the world has perhaps ever witnessed'. Equally unparalleled, however, was the co-existence of so much suffering in one portion of the people, with so much prosperity in another; of unbounded private wealth, with unceasing public penury . . . of the utmost freedom consistent with order, ever yet existing upon earth, with a degree of discontent which keeps the nation constantly on the verge of insurrection.
>
> The nation had come to accept 'this extraordinary combination . . . as unavoidable'. If such vastly different conditions of living were accepted as 'unavoidable', so also were the different types of education (Lawson and Silver, 1973: 270-71).

The question in the nineteenth-century was never whether the education for the poor should be the same as the education appropriate for their social superiors — the question was whether the lower orders needed education at all.

The House of Lords would reject any measure on education that was sent up to it; and it was very unlikely that the government of the day would introduce an Education bill. Melbourne, though a Whig, had the greatest dislike of any social legislation, especially of education. He thought it a pity 'to bother the poor'. They were much better left alone. His various pronouncements on education were all hostile to it (Sturt, 1967: 76).

The contrast between lower and upper class education may best be seen in two nineteenth-century official reports: the Newcastle Report (1861) and the Clarendon Report (1864). The terms of reference of the Newcastle Commission were to enquire into 'the present state of popular education and to consider and report on what measures, if any, are required for the extension of sound and cheap elementary instruction to all classes of the people'. As a result of this commission the elementary curriculum was fixed as basic skills in the 3 Rs together with religious instruction. It was repeatedly stressed that elementary education should not be too ambitious, and should not give the lower orders ideas above their station.

Three years later the Clarendon Report (1864) gave a totally different picture of the curriculum regarded as suitable for upper class pupils in Endowed Schools or Public Schools. The contrast between the elementary pupil leaving school at age 10 or 11 and the public school boy leaving at age 18 or 19 was not simply a question of duration, it was a deliberate policy of maintaining a difference in quality of education.

I used these two reports in 1973 (*Social Change, Educational Theory and Curriculum Planning*) to illustrate the changes which had taken place in English society since the 1860s. That much is obvious — but perhaps what we also need to stress is the *survival* of these attitudes rather than their gradual decline.

They certainly survived throughout the nineteenth century: between the years 1864 to 1868 The Schools Enquiry Commission (The Taunton Commission) was investigating secondary education. The Report recommended that there should be three separate grades of secondary school corresponding roughly with the social ranking of pupils. Secondary education was almost entirely thought of in terms of middle-class children: First Grade Secondary Schools being suitable for upper middle-class children; Second Grade Schools for middle-class children; and in the Third Grade Schools there would be a mixture of lower middle-class children and a small proportion of respectable upper working-class children to be given the kind of education described as 'a clerk's education'. This was a clear expression of the policy of different schools and different curricula for different levels of social strata. There was no suggestion that the question of *ability* should be considered. As regards curriculum it was recommended that First Grade Schools should have a school leaving age of 18 or 19, the curriculum consisting largely of Latin and Greek with some mathematics, some science and a modern language. These pupils would normally proceed to a university if they wanted to. Second Grade Schools should have a leaving age of 16 or 17, the curriculum consisting of Latin (but no Greek) and two foreign languages, English and science. These pupils would be equipped to enter such professions as the army, law, or civil engineering. Third Grade Schools would have a school leaving age of 14 or 15, the curriculum consisting of 'reading, writing and arithmetic – a clerk's education'.

The vast majority of working-class children in the nineteenth century had little possibility of reaching secondary school. For most of them the best they would get was the kind of elementary education which was set up following the Newcastle Report and which was eventually tidied up in the

1870 Act. H. G. Wells, who had been both a pupil and a teacher in elementary schools, was later to comment bitterly on the class basis of education as enshrined in the 1870 Education Act. 'An Act to educate the lower classes for employment on lower class lines, and with specially-trained, inferior teachers.' (Quoted by Lowndes, 1937: 5).

Thus, from the beginning elementary education was seen as a deliberately inferior kind of education for the lower orders. Not only did it begin as inferior education, it was deliberately kept inferior by such devices as the 1862 Revised Code (which effectively confined the elementary curriculum to the 3 Rs) and the Cockerton Judgement (1899) which declared that any attempts to enrich the elementary curriculum were illegal.

The nineteenth-century background to segregation based on class is clear. But the point I want to emphasize is that these attitudes have survived throughout the twentieth-century. Despite a succession of education Acts, which have apparently extended educational opportunities to all sections of the community, I suggest there is still a general acceptance of the idea that it is reasonable to segregate children from different social backgrounds for educational purposes.

Many people have assumed that the battle was fought and won in the second half of the nineteenth-century century. This belief springs from such liberal utilitarian successes as reforms of army and civil service recruitment. Entrance of potential officers to Sandhurst and Woolwich was made dependent on examinations in the 1850s, as was recruitment to most civil service posts after the Northcote-Trevelyan Report (1853). But our interest is not so much in the victory as in the fact that the reforms were bitterly resisted. It may be worth examining some of these arguments and asking whether such beliefs have completely disappeared from twentieth-century consciousness. The system of 'patronage' had many defenders including the novelist Anthony Trollope who felt that it was more important that the higher ranks in the civil service should be filled by honourable gentlemen rather than upstarts who were merely clever. The idea that breeding was more important than the doubtful quality of ability was widely held:

> The Report (of the Northcote-Trevelyan Commission 1853) met with the usual type of objection. It was said that clever men were not necessarily trustworthy; that an examination was not a good test of 'character'; that candidates of ability would not care to sit for an examination (Woodward, 1954: 599).

Have such views completely disappeared? Apparently not: we are told by students of political sociology that so-called 'deference voters' today still prefer to elect upper-class parliamentary candidates; there is also a good deal of evidence that class is more important than attainment or ability in a wide range of top jobs – in the city for example. (A. Sampson, 1971), or for judges and civil servants (D. Boyd, 1973).

It is a mistake to assume that in the twentieth-century only conservatives and reactionaries hold social elitist ideas about education. Throughout the twentieth-century there have been intermittent debates about 'culture' and many so-called 'liberals' have expressed influential views about the need to preserve an aristocracy or a minority class, who alone could guarantee the production of worthwhile art and literature. Much of the discussion among the Bloomsbury Group on 'art for art's sake' was couched in such terms. One extremely influential book of this kind was Clive Bell's *Civilization* (1928). Bell argued that civilization was in danger of being destroyed by many aspects of modern philistine society; but it could, he suggested, be preserved by a small group of superior individuals ('a civilized nucleus') who would not only cherish the best in our civilization, but also, by their example, spread a little sweetness and light down to the masses. Central to this idea was the need for a *leisure class* to be maintained by society:

> ...a leisured class is essential... the men and women who are to compose that nucleus from which radiates civilization must have security, leisure, economic freedom, and liberty to think, feel and experiment. If the community wants civilization it must pay for it. It must support a leisured class as it supports schools and universities, museums and picture galleries. This implies inequality — inequality as a means to good. On inequality all civilizations have stood (Bell, 1928: 208-9).

In fairness to Bell, it must be admitted that he did not necessarily recommend that the leisured class *should* be hereditary, only that it *could* be. If this were a bizarre, isolated point of view there would be no point in mentioning it. It is important, however, because the central idea has survived: that there are some people who by reason of their birth or breeding have certain potentialities which the masses (even the intelligent ones) do not and cannot share. There is a clear line drawn by Bell between the civilized 'us' and the barbarous 'them' which is still present in much discussion of education whether in the limited sense of schooling or more generally concerning radio and television 'tastes'. F. R. Leavis and some of his followers have sometimes taken this line which has had serious effects on the teaching of English.

An even more extreme view, and probably even more influential, is closer to us in time. T. S. Eliot's *Notes Towards the Definition of Culture* was published in 1948 and has been reprinted and discussed very frequently since then. Eliot also felt that for a worthwhile community to be preserved it was essential to have an elite. And, unlike Bell, Eliot felt that there was no possible alternative to an elite based on class. Although he admitted that in the past there have been members of the dominant class 'conspicuously deficient in "culture" ' he persisted in his argument that the elite must be a 'social', that is a class-based, elite:

> In an elite composed of individuals who find their way into it solely for their individual pre-eminence, the differences of background will be so great, that they will be united only by their common interests, and separated by everything else. An elite must therefore be attached to *some* class, whether higher or lower: but so long as there are classes at all it is likely to be the dominant class that attracts this elite to itself. What would happen in a classless society — which is much more difficult to envisage than people think — brings us into the area of conjecture. There are, however, some guesses which seem to me worth venturing.
>
> The primary channel of transmission of culture is the family: no man wholly escapes from the kind, or wholly surpasses the degree, of culture which he acquired from his early environment (Eliot, 1948: 42-43).

Eliot also had a good deal more to say than Bell about education. He argued that education should help to preserve 'class', and to select the elite from that class (p. 100). Public Schools were excellent means of educating the social elite (not the intellectual elite) for this reason. Education of some kind should be provided for all children, but we would need to be very careful not to destroy the class system by education or other social means. 'The disintegration of class has induced the expansion of envy, which provides ample fuel for the flames of "equal opportunity".'

Eliot's views have been frequently attacked and found wanting. For example, Bottomore (1964) criticized Eliot for assuming that the family is the only possible agency for transmitting culture, whereas there are plenty of historical examples of alternatives. Raymond Williams (1958) went further and accused Eliot of using arguments which were inconsistent, lacking in logical coherence and even verging on the dishonest (Culture and Society, p. 228-29). But, despite these criticisms and refutations, Eliot's version of social elitism is still a powerful factor in current educational debate, for example in the Black Papers.

Perhaps the most influential exponent today of the social elitist view is Professor G. Bantock. The importance of Bantock is partly that he represents not the upper class cultural superiority view of Eliot, but the obverse of the coin: namely the view that the working classes are incapable of benefiting from the same kind of education as their social superiors. Bantock does not argue, as a nineteenth-century Whig would have, that the lower orders have no *right* to this kind of superior education; merely that their cultural background makes a normal conventional curriculum inappropriate for the masses. This is very important because it is precisely this assumption which may be responsible for a good deal of working-class under-achievement in schools today.

Bantock derives his argument partly from Eliot and the Leavisite tradition of English teaching already referred to, and partly from his admiration for the views of D. H. Lawrence. Like Eliot and Bell, Bantock's major error is that he exaggerates the differences between high culture and mass culture (even if we accept the validity of these terms at all), and thus he badly underestimates the potentialities of the majority of the population. Bantock argues that the masses are historically and psychologically ill-equipped to deal with traditional culture which is a literary culture, where the 'folk' tradition is oral rather than written. He puts forward an interesting, but unconvincing, argument that literature encourages introspection and has become a means of fostering individualism and privacy. Thus, one of the dominant themes of English literature is the search for personal identity, a concept which is unknown in primitive and folk cultures. The majority of people, according to Bantock, have lived emotional − not intellectual − existences, and educationists should recognize this fact. Therefore Bantock recommends two kinds of education − a literary, logical, intellectual curriculum for a small minority, and a totally different curriculum for the majority which would include basic literary skills but would concentrate on education of the emotions and senses. Bantock claims that popular education has failed largely because it has attempted to initiate everyone into a minority culture. He quotes with approval D. H. Lawrence's statement 'the great mass of humanity should never learn to read and write − never', although he admits that modern industrial society now makes a certain level of literacy necessary for all.

Thus we have a new kind of justification for educational segregation based on class: not that the upper classes have superior needs and expectations but that the lower classes are incapable of benefiting from the same kind of education as their social superiors. This has been shown to be very important in our schools in a variety of ways. Many teachers behave as though the assumption that working-class children are of low ability or low motivation is a correct assumption even if they pay lip-service to equality of opportunity. Halsey and Gardner's work (1953) in London grammar schools showed that teachers rated working-class pupils lower not only on their academic records but on personality characteristics associated with school success; teachers generally felt that working-class pupils were less likely to profit from a grammar school education than middle-class boys. Similarly Himmelweit (1954) showed that grammar school teachers tended to give working-class pupils lower personality ratings on a whole range of criteria from general behaviour in school to industriousness. More recently Nell Keddie's study of a comprehensive school showed that teachers' expectation of pupils' achievement was partly related to their social class background. If we make the connection between these kinds of studies and what we now know about the importance of teachers' expectations and pupil achievement then it is quite clear that we have a very serious situation indeed. Yates (1966: 137) has shown that pupils 'are obliging creatures and are very inclined to produce the standard of work that their elders regard as appropriate'. The classic study about pupil expectation and pupil performance was of course *Pygmalion in the Classroom* by Rosenthal and Jacobson (1968). Despite the methodological difficulties and some of the criticisms which have been made about the statistical techniques used in this study there is at least a strong suspicion that teachers' attitudes can be altered and that teachers' expectations of pupils' performance have a powerful effect on their actual classroom achievement. There are numerous other studies which show similar results although in slightly different contexts. For example, the study by Marburger (1963) concludes: 'The teacher who expects achievement, who has hope for the educability of his pupils, indeed conveys this through every nuance and subtlety of his behaviour. The teacher who conveys hopelessness for the educability of his children usually does so without ever really verbalising such an attitude — at least not in front of his pupils' (p. 306). In this connection the most detailed study of this kind which has been carried out in the UK has been that of Burstall (1968). Clare Burstall found that one of the most powerful factors in determining whether children would succeed in learning French in the primary school or not was the attitude of the teacher. Those teachers who had a strong belief in French in the primary school tended to have success across the ability range of pupils; those who did not have any such belief had comparative failure across the ability range. Burstall makes a general point as a result of this kind of finding which has particular application to the problem of teachers' attitudes and the social class or home background of the pupils:

> In a complex of factors determining a pupil's achievement, it must surely be recognised that the teacher's attitudes and expectations are of paramount importance. We readily accept that curriculum change cannot be effected without the whole-hearted involvement of the teacher; we are perhaps less ready to recognise that changes in the curriculum, no matter how far-reaching, will have little effect on the pupil from whom the teacher expects — and obtains — a low level of achievement.

There would appear therefore to be a vicious circle operating with teachers and their working-class pupils: first of all teachers expect working-class children to fail or to have lower achievement; second, many working-class pupils pick up this expectation message from the teachers and then fulfil this expectation by their under-achievement; finally teachers are reinforced in their assumption about working-class ineducability. Martin Trow has made the same kind of observation in the US in connection with the problem of racial minorities (Trow, 1968, quoted by Pidgeon, 1970). On the other hand, there is no evidence of a convincing kind in support of the social elitist point of view. There are, of course, statistical studies which show a correlation between social class and IQ. But apart from the methodological difficulties, and the problems of interpreting such results, these kinds of statistical correlation would certainly not justify segregating working-class and middle-class pupils, and treating them differently in their educational process. Part of the difficulty here may be a confusion between statistical generalizations and the performance and treatment of individual children. Even if it were established that there was a much greater correlation between social class and IQ, the overlap would be so great as to argue against segregation; the same arguments apply here as for the desegregation of schools in the US. Unfortunately it is unnecessary to exclude working-class children from schools or classes in order to sell them short in education. Given the assumptions that many teachers have about social class or background (often reinforced by ill-digested sociological texts) many pupils will be conditioned to failure or, as Martin Trow expressed it, become the victims of 'the culture of defeat'.

Social elitism as a doctrine is dangerous in two ways. First, at a time when the pendulum is swinging to the right, social elitism might be used to justify policies of a reactionary kind — for example, bolstering up various forms of independent education by means of voucher systems, etc. The second danger is much more serious because it is not open to scrutiny. It is that teachers, consciously or unconsciously, are still influenced by social elitist assumptions that class or home background limits educability — or worse still that the majority of children are ineducable. Much more needs to be done to attack the false doctrine of social elitism at both levels. It is difficult to see how this question of attitudes in education can be tackled in isolation from more general elitist attitudes surviving in our society. It is also difficult to see how the vexed question of public schools and other independent schools can be avoided much longer. It is a clear case of injustice because it allows people to have a superior education (superior in some respects) for the irrelevant reason of possessing parents who have enough money to pay fees. It used to be thought that this question would gradually wither away, but all the signs are against this. In 1973 David Boyd published a study (*Elites and Their Education*) which showed that the social and political changes that have taken place since the war have done almost nothing to diminish the close connection between public schools, Oxford and Cambridge Universities, and the elite professions (members of the elite professions being, in this study, ambassadors in the foreign service, judges, Church of England bishops, senior officers in the armed services, senior civil servants, and senior staff in the clearing banks). The fact that there is such a connection between public schools and top jobs may have serious implications for the economy.

> When Hitler's Panzer Division crashed through the rifle and bayonet-equipped British troups in Belgium, and gained the Channel ports for war on Britain, the public school system received its reward for being fifty years out-of-date. This is not to say that public schools are wholly useless, or that public school men are wholly without merit. Everyone knows the public school virtues, self-control, courage, endurance, loyalty. But unfortunately none of these qualities by themselves are of any use against a tank. (T. C. Worsley, quoted by Boyd, 1973: 38).

If Worsley were writing this now instead of in 1941 he might attribute some of our inefficiency in industry to the fact that too many top jobs in industry as well as the elite professions still are allocated on the basis of the old school tie and the old boy network rather than selecting the best man for the job. But this is not the major point. As far as this book is concerned the important issue is that so long as there are public schools with a better staff-pupil ratio than state schools can afford, and so long as public schools produce the goods in terms of good jobs in the City, etc. then the question of social justice in education cannot be separated from social justice in society at large, particularly the question of access to certain kinds of occupation. This is in itself an admission that is difficult to promote social justice in education without going some way towards eliminating social injustice in the wider community. In this respect the whole question of heredity and privilege is important both as an issue in its own right, and for the effect that this kind of social structure has on the teaching profession and their attitudes towards working-class children. In a society in which privilege is respectable and deeply entrenched, it is asking a great deal to expect teachers to be completely free of the assumptions held by the rest of society. Nevertheless if we recognize that this kind of problem exists then something can be done about improving teachers' awareness of the problem. But this should, of course, be recognized as a palliative rather than a cure for what Tawney described as 'the hereditary curse upon English education'. When Tawney's *Equality* was reissued in paperback version in 1964 Richard Titmuss wrote an introduction in which he stated his belief that the basic content of *Equality* was still very relevant in the 1960s, but he also made this point:

> We thus delude ourselves if we think that we can equalise the social distribution of life chances by expanding educational opportunities while millions of children live in slums without baths, decent lavatories, leisure facilities, room to explore and the space to dream. Nor do we achieve with any permanency a fairer distribution of rewards and a society less sharply divided by class and status by simply narrowing the difference in cash earnings among men during certain limited periods of their lives (pp. 11-12).

The point is that social justice in education must be seen as part of a wider problem, but the kind of evidence that Titmuss goes on to quote supports my thesis that the problem is a very deep-rooted one. Although many teachers might be horrified at the suggestion that they are social elitists at heart, in fact the structure of society makes it very difficult for them not to betray some of these attitudes in their classroom behaviour. It is for this reason that social elitism needs to be attacked as a doctrine as well as treated as part of a much more general social problem.

INTELLECTUAL ELITISM OR MERITOCRACY

It might be true to say that whereas social elitism was the dominant educational ideology of the nineteenth century, intellectual elitism dominates twentieth-century educational thinking. Many aspects of social elitism are still powerful in our schools, however, and there still tends to be much confusion between these two overlapping ideologies. In England it is difficult to have intellectual elitism in a pure form. What is much more likely is a mixture of social and intellectual elitism — probably confused still further by the package being wrapped up in some egalitarian terminology. By intellectual elitism I mean separating children into 'types' not by their social rank but by their supposed intellectual type. There are two main assumptions behind this idea of intellectual elitism. The first is that there are *identifiable* psychological types; the second is that these different types need different *kinds* of education — preferably in separate schools, certainly in separate classes or teaching groups. In opposing this kind of elitism I am not, of course, suggesting that all children have the same educational potential, or that intelligence is not an important factor in education. What I wish to dispute is the assumption that it is sensible to try to group complex differences into just two or three categories or types of pupil; I also want to dispute that even if it were possible to categorize children in this way, that different types of children should be given a different *kind* of education. A wide variety of approaches and teaching methods is very desirable but that is quite different from categorizing some children as 'non-academic' and giving them an inferior curriculum. The Plowden Report was making more or less this point in its discussion of streaming. The Committee came to the conclusion that they were opposed to streaming not because they thought all primary children were the same, but because they were *so* different that to stream 35 children into one class and treat them identically was an over-simplified and unsatisfactory solution. I want to pursue this argument into secondary education and say that it is a dangerous over-simplification to think of individual differences in terms of two schools, or three bands, or nine streams. It is also true that in some respects we should think of what *all* children have in common, as well as to take good notice of their differences.

The transition from social elitism to an aristocracy of talent was one of the most interesting features of nineteenth-century social change. The philosophical radicals such as Bentham, James Mill and John Stuart Mill were mainly middle-class intellectuals who resented the power and influence of the aristocracy. Utilitarian philosophy and the economic theory of Adam Smith provided them with an ideological basis for advocating certain kinds of social change. The move 'from patronage to competition' was to a large extent identifiable with the growth of examinations which was discussed in Chapter 2. Public examinations were favoured as a reliable means and a just means of identifying talent (and presumably demonstrating the incompetence of those who failed the examinations; for example, the younger sons of aristocrats and gentlemen). This general tendency to identify talent by means of examinations and to select people for posts by this method had indirect as well as direct influences on the schools. Schools gradually became places where talent was produced or fostered and they became agencies of selection as well as education. Some schools, including a few of the great public schools, introduced special classes for those who wished to enter for the public examinations such as the army and the civil service. They may have been taught separately from other pupils of the same age, but this was more to cope with the different syllabus required for the examinations than because they were necessarily thought of as different types of intellect or ability.

In the elementary schools, however, the 'ladder' of opportunity was fostered by Robert Lowe and others in the second half of the nineteenth century. The idea here was certainly that the more intelligent pupils of any social class should be identified as early as possible, and encouraged to climb out of the elementary school into the secondary school by passing a competitive examination. Although this was the beginning of the idea of a scholarship ladder from elementary school to university, in practice there was little opportunity for such mobility in the nineteenth century. The most that an able working-class pupil could hope for was the apprenticeship route from pupil-teacher to training college by means of a Queen's Scholarship Examination.

In the middle-class schools, examinations were increasingly used as a means of identifying superior *attainment* but probably not *intelligence*. Much of the argument in favour of examinations at this time was concerned with the need to provide incentives for youths who were thought of as naturally idle, but as the nineteenth-century drew on there was increasing attention paid to the idea of examinations as a means of identifying the more able rather than the merely hard-working pupil. Although the word was not invented until 1958, the idea of *meritocracy* was gaining ground in liberal circles: i.e. that selection for important positions should be based on a combination of ability and hard work. To select men for jobs on the basis of merit rather than their social connections was, as we saw in Chapter 2, bitterly opposed in some quarters.

The essence of the idea of meritocracy as defined by Michael Young (1958) was that

$$IQ + Effort = Merit$$

(i.e. both natural ability and hard work are desirable and necessary). Although the notion of IQ is a twentieth-century invention, the idea of high ability matched by an equivalent amount of effort producing a serious candidate for advancement was certainly developed by the second half of the nineteenth-century, and Robert Lowe himself was a good example of the meritocratic ideal which was developing.

So far so good. The use of examinations in this way was part of the social change marking the transition from a landed aristocratic society to an industrial society. Birth or breeding was ceasing to be so important, and ability becoming more important. In the nineteenth-century there was no provision for separate teaching for the different kinds of ability within schools. Social class was still the means of segregating pupils into different schools. Even after the 1902 Act which encouraged local authorities to set up their own Secondary Schools, these were thought of as middle-class schools which might be open to a few clever working-class boys. At this stage the assumption was still strongly that secondary education was appropriate for all middle-class pupils (or all who could afford to pay) but only for *some* working-class pupils — the highly talented who could be excused fees on account of their very superior abilities.

Hence there was the need for selecting some working-class pupils in the elementary schools, taking them out of those schools and sending them to secondary schools. It is this process of selection which is the key factor in most twentieth-century disputes on education.

The idea of the 'ladder of opportunity' has confused the real issue of universal secondary education ever since. When educationists should have been discussing questios of *what* to teach and *how* to teach it, most of the debate since 1944 has been on the irrelevant question of '*who* should be educated?'. This red herring of how to *select* children for secondary education has dominated discussions of education, including discussions within the Labour Party as we shall see in Chapter 7.

During most of the nineteenth-century the distinction between elementary education and secondary education had been carefully preserved. In 1899 the Cockerton Judgment finally closed the door to the idea of improving elementary education and making it a genuine kind of popular education available to all pupils. Morant (another early meritocrat) advocated keeping the two systems firmly apart. He believed that secondary education was for leadership, and that the function of a good secondary school was to produce the most efficient and the most able leaders available. His views were behind the 1902 Education Act which encouraged the development of state maintained secondary or grammar schools. These were fee-paying schools, but after 1907 one-quarter of the places were required to be free for 'scholar-ship' winners. By 1920 40 percent of the places were free. In 1932 these free places for a time became 'special places' with payment according to a means test. But some local authorities made all places free, and by 1939 there were about 10 percent of the age group 11-15 in maintained secondary schools and of that 10 percent the majority (about four-fifths) paid no fees.

The scholarship ladder had been established, but it became increasingly clear in the 1920s and 1930s that working-class pupils were not getting their fair share of the special places or free places in the secondary schools. It was this kind of social injustice which served to divert attention away from the real problem of education for all. The problem of 'fairness' was seen as a question of securing equality of opportunity for a minority of children to get out of the elementary schools at age 11, whereas the real problem was to ensure an adequate education for *all* children up to the age of 14 (or later on 15 and 16). This problem of 'fair selection' may be seen either as an inevitable stage on the road to greater social justice or as a misleading dead end, and one which has served to distort educational debate ever since.

It is difficult to know how much blame can be attached to early twentieth-century educationists and reforming politicians for failing to avoid the pitfalls of a segregated system of education. For example, R. H. Tawney in 1922 edited a policy document for the Labour Party called *Secondary Education for All*. The title was, in retrospect, more optimistic than its detailed recommendations. So entrenched by this time was the idea of a divided system that even Tawney and the other members of the Labour Party accepted without question the idea that at the age of 11 different 'types' of pupil, i.e. different levels of intellectual ability, should be allocated to different kinds of school: the policy of segregation plus 'parity of esteem' was established. It is easy to be wise after the event, but maybe it should have been possible to have seen then, that it is impossible to select a minority of children for superior schools without appearing to condemn the majority to an inferior kind of education. This is especially so when we remember that at this time so much attention was being paid to devising tests which would be fair in selecting the superior intellects from the inferior.

After the 1907 Regulations had required local authorities to provide 25 percent of the secondary school places for scholarship winners, it was necessary to have an examination system to select the most deserving. This generally took the form of tests in English, arithmetic, history and geography. Teachers, still smarting under the after-effects of the Revised Code of 1862 and the payment by results system, complained that the rigid and unimaginative examinations which were set restricted the development of the curriculum. This led to the recommendation that the scholarship examination should be limited to English and arithmetic. A number of educationists became increasingly dissatisfied with the inadequacy of this kind of examination, however, and in 1919 Bradford Education Committee began to use tests devised by Cyril Burt. At about the same time in Northumberland Professor Godfrey Thompson was a member of the education committee and he was also interested in psychological testing as a means of discovering able children in schools who, he suspected, were not really doing themselves justice in conventional examinations. The aim of psychologists at this time was to compensate for the advantages of a large school or better schools and individual coaching. They wanted to devise a selection procedure that would give equal chances to all candidates. The task was to set tests which would not favour the prepared candidate at the expense of the ill-prepared or unprepared pupil. Psychologists were very optimistic about the use of intelligence tests in this respect. It should perhaps be stressed that the psychologists producing IQ tests at the time, were often motivated by 'democratic' ideas: for example, Professor Godfrey Thompson defended the tests in this way 'These psychological tests favour the gifted boy with poor advantages, rather than the rich boy with gifted tutors, and are therefore essentially a democratic method of selection' (*Newcastle Daily Journal,* 27 November

1921). The motives were good but the result in the long run was unfortunate.

The more time and energy that psychologists spent on producing tests, the more they were inclined to believe their own propaganda. A weakness that was always present in the system had to be glossed over. But the weakness was an enormous one. Intelligence tests were based on the assumption that intelligence, like height, had a normal curve of distribution. Just as there are a few very tall people, a few very short and the majority somewhere in the middle, so it was assumed that there should be similar proportions of very intelligent, average and below average individuals. If you measure the height of all adult men in England you get a distribution something like the graph shown in Figure 1. The important point to note is that there are no gaps: you will get men whose height is 6′ 6″, 6′ 5″ and so on down to 5′ 5″ or so. The distribution is continuous, and the same kind of distribution is assumed for intelligence. On any 'good' intelligence test, you should get high scorers, low scorers and average scorers, but without there being any way of deciding exactly where the cut-off point should be for deciding whether anyone should be regarded as superior or not. It is easy to work out the average (in intelligence or height) but there is no way of deciding whether it is right to call someone whose height is 5′ 9″ 'tall'. Would 5′ 10″ be more appropriate? Or 5′ 9½″? They are all above average, but how much above average would they have to be to deserve the title 'tall'? Exactly the same problem existed for those in the above average intelligence category. An arbitrary point had to be decided to allocate pupils to grammar schools. Someone who scored 163 marks out of 200 on a test might go to grammar school but not someone who scored 162. In practice the point was usually determined by the number of places available in the grammar schools rather than any particular merit being attached to a specific mark on a scale; the cut-off point would differ from one year to the next and from one district to another. I do not wish to embark upon an attack on the concept of intelligence and the practice of IQ testing. This has been done many times before (see, for example, Simon, 1971). My point is simply that even if someone accepted psychologists' claims for the validity and reliability of IQ tests, this would *not* commit him to believing in two or three (or more) types of child. And even if − despite the evidence − someone does believe that there are three 'types' of child, this does not commit him to three different *kinds* of education.

Figure 1

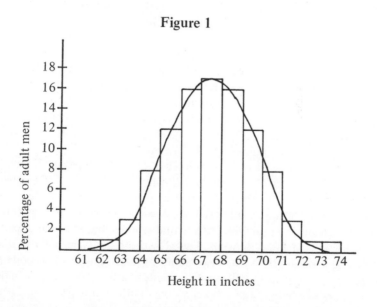

Height in inches

When I say that psychologists came to believe their own propaganda I mean that they began to overstate their ability to select accurately. By the time some of them were giving evidence to official government committees such as the Hadow Committee in 1926, they were claiming not simply to be able to put together useful tests which could be used to select (fairly accurately) the top 8 or 10 percent of the ability range as requested in any particular year (it would inevitably vary from time to time and place to place), the psychologists were now claiming to be able to identify distinct *types of ability* at the age of 11. Evidence of the exaggerated claims of psychologists may be seen in an interesting way in the Introduction to the Hadow Report. Not only were psychologists claiming at this time to be able to distinguish types of ability, they were also making very strange generalizations about the nature of children, and in particular the 11-12-year-old age group:

> There is a tide which begins to rise in the veins of youth at the age of eleven or twelve. It is called by the name of adolescence. If that tide can be taken at the flood, and a new voyage begun in the strength and along the flow of its current, we think that it will 'move on to fortune'. We therefore propose that all children should be transferred, at the age of eleven or twelve, from the junior or primary school either to schools of the type now called secondary, or to schools (whether selective or non-selective) of the type which is now called central, or to senior and separate departments of existing elementary schools. Here however we are concerned with the growth — which has begun already, and which we desire greatly to accelerate — of selective and non-selective central schools, and of senior departments in elementary schools. This growth, in our view, will run side by side with, but in no sense counter to, the growth of secondary schools; and while it will differ in kind, it will not be inferior in its promise or quality. The central schools and senior departments, like the secondary schools, will give a humane and general education. It will be shorter in its duration; it will terminate at the end of three or four years; but it will be directed, as long as it lasts, to the general fostering of mental power. Two methods, which will differentiate them to some extent from secondary schools, will generally be

followed in central schools and senior departments. One will be the method of practical instruction and manual work, on which we set high hopes, believing that there are many children who think as it were with their hands and profit greatly by a method of instruction which follows the natural bent of their capacity. Another will be the method of giving a trend and a bias, which for want of a better word we may call by the name 'realistic', to the general course of studies . . . .

On the question of the skill of psychologists in selecting children for three different kinds of school the Spens Report in 1938 was even more explicit: 'We are informed that, with few exceptions, it is possible at a very early age to predict with some degree of accuracy the ultimate level of a child's intellectual powers.'

To be fair to the psychologists some of them did complain that the Spens Report had overstated the case. But by then the damage had been done: it was popularly accepted that there were different kinds of ability, that these different types could be selected by means of a test, and that they should be given a different kind of school curriculum. The assumption that children should be given different kinds of curriculum was of course completely unsupported by any evidence.

Unfortunately the ensuing arguments about *testing* served to draw the fire of educational reformers and to distract them from a much more important task — namely to demolish the assumption that even if there were separate types of ability and even if we had tests good enough to select fairly, that the different types really needed quite different kinds of education. In other words those who objected to the lack of fairness in the selection process mounted their attack on the procedures of selection rather than on the *principle* of selection. Unfortunately this wrong target continued to be aimed at for a very long time.

That tendency can be seen clearly in the work of socio-logists and others in the 1920s and 1930s. The tendency was also kept going by the fact that there seemed to be an ever increasing demand for more secondary school places and that since there was unfulfilled demand there was probably in-justice in the selection of people for the scarce places. It was the inequality of access to secondary schools which occupied the Labour Party and most reformers in the inter-war years rather than the much more basic but much more important question about the content of education for the whole popu-lation. Gray and Moshinsky (1938), for example, accepted the principle that educational success had to be related to ability or natural endowment, and proceeded to demonstrate the gross inequality of educational opportunity especially the fact that highly intelligent working-class children were under-represented in secondary schools and higher education. Left-wing reformers, including most of the Labour Party and the TUC, saw the problem of 'fairness' in education simply as a question of access to particular kinds of educational institu-tions, grammar schools in particular. In the 1930s, however, a few voices were raised against the idea of selection; for example, the Labour MP Lees-Smith who stated that 'We talk of class distinctions and how to get rid of them, but a new class distinction is arising, namely the distinction between those who pass an academic examination at the age of eleven and those who do not pass it.' (Quoted by Harold Silver, 1973: 5.)

The majority view inside the Labour Party, however, was that equality of opportunity meant making selection as fair as possible, particularly from a social class point of view. Another voice making a plea for social justice of a more basic kind was that of Clarke (1943):

For secondary education in England is suffering severely, as the Spens Report again recognises, from a grave lack of genuine educational diversity. The newer schools, staffed in many cases by men bred in the old tradition, and, often under the influence of governors of the same cultural stock, have tended to follow only too faithfully the model of the ancient schools, public and grammar. In this they have not been discouraged if not actively encouraged by their lower middle class and upper working class clientele. In British colonies, especially in Africa, strong suspicion is revealed of any attempt to adapt secondary education to local needs and conditions as concealing a design to rob aspiring pupils and parents of the hope of achieving 'caste'. The same suspicion was strong until recently even in England, towards attempts to work out special secondary curricula suitable for the education of girls. Now today it is active among the classes of the population whose hopes of achieving status are founded upon the new facilities that were opened up by the Act of 1902. Overwhelmingly the driving force is the desire for status rather than for education as such.

But even Fred Clarke saw the solution to this problem as separate schools with cross connections rather than a single route. He confused the need for educational diversity with the need for separate institutions which would inevitably become hierarchical in their differentiation.

The argument about kinds of ability and different curricula was carried to its furthest extreme in the Norwood Report (1943) where it was claimed that it was possible to identify three types of child: the Report claimed that there were three quite distinct types of pupil. One of them was a pupil who was 'interested in learning for its own sake', such a pupil apparently was able to 'grasp an argument or follow a piece of connected reasoning', he was 'interested in causes'. This was, of course, the grammar school type of pupil suited for the learned professions or business posts. The second Norwood type was the pupil 'whose interests and abilities lie markedly in the field of applied science or applied art'. This pupil was interested in mechanical things, and although his abilities showed 'uncanny insight' in this respect the 'subtleties of language construction are too delicate for him'. Such a pupil might have unusual or moderate intelligence, and they would take up crafts, engineering, agriculture and the like. There was a third group of pupil interested in concrete things rather than ideas: things as they are rather than in the past or in 'the slow disentanglement of causes or movements'. 'His mind must turn its knowledge or its curiosity to immediate test; and his test is essentially practical.' 'Because he is interested only in the moment he may be incapable of a long series of connected steps; relevance to present concerns is the only way of awakening interest, abstractions mean little to him.' Apart from being the justification for three kinds of school, this was also supposed to be a basis for parity of esteem, but the condescension obvious in the descriptions of the technical and modern pupils clearly did not augur well for the post-war tripartite system which rested on the doctrine that the three types of schools would be different but equal. The Norwood Report continued with a description of the three types of curriculum which would be necessary to meet the needs of these three quite different types of child.

This grossly over-simplified view of children's abilities was vigorously denied by Cyril Burt (1943) and other psychologists. But by then the myth was well-established. And the 1944 Education Act was interpreted by the Ministry of Education officials in much the same way as their colleagues had interpreted the psychological evidence to the Norwood Committee, namely as a justification for the tripartite system rather than the common school.

In this, as in many other respects, it was not the scientific evidence or the opinions of experts which really mattered, but the over-simplified view which had been created in the minds of the population as a whole, and of teachers and educational administrators in particular. During the 1930s there was certainly an official acceptance by the Board of Education (and after the war by the Ministry of Education) of the intellectual elitist point of view. Whether this was the result of a simplistic interpretation of the ideas of psychologists which were in themselves occasionally exaggerated, or whether this was the result of a policy, conscious or unconscious, on the part of upper middle-class officials to protect their own vested interests, we do not know.

It was the Norwood Report which 'transformed tripartitism from a proposal into a doctrine' (Dent, 1949: 137). It was also responsible for moving public examinations away from the idea of a common core to the principle of single subject examinations — but that is another story! It could have been worse: in 1944 when the Education Act was passed there was a distinct possibility that tripartitism might have been written in to the Act as the only way of organizing secondary education for all, but teachers and others within the Labour Party engineered a protest from the National Executive. Alice Bacon claimed that 'As a result of our deputation and others, the 1944 Education Act did not have the term "three types of secondary schools" . . . which left the way open for the comprehensive or common secondary school' (Report of the Labour Party Conference 1950, pp. 92-95 quoted by Banks, 1955: 133). Thus, the wording of the Act itself was neutral on this point, leaving it to LEAs to decide whether 'secondary education for all' meant in one school or in three (or eventually, in most cases, either in secondary modern schools or secondary grammar schools). The influence of the Ministry of Education officials at this stage is most interesting. In May 1945 a pamphlet called *The Nation's Schools* was issued; it advised LEAs that the tripartite division of schools into secondary grammar, technical or modern was the most appropriate way of interpreting the 1944 Act. The timing of this pamphlet was important since it was issued *before* the Labour victory in the 1945 general election. Ellen Wilkinson, the then Labour Minister of Education, was dominated by policies previously formulated by her civil servants. Despite protests from within the Labour Party she refused to disown or to withdraw the pamphlet which had been authorized by the previous administration. She merely went ahead with the new circular *The Organisation of Secondary Education* which was issued in December 1945. This official circular did not exclude the possibility of comprehensive schools, but showed a strong preference for the tripartite system. This interesting episode showed very clearly that the Ministry of Education officials still thought of grammar schools as providing the only real education of a secondary kind, and that this was education of a select few. Whether they were influenced by the pseudo-psychology contained in the Spens and Norwood Reports or simply by their own prejudices remains, as yet, a matter of speculation. The patronizing attitude towards other kinds of secondary education in both the pamphlet and the circular in 1945 was quite clear.

Most LEAs followed the Ministry of Education lead and organized secondary education along tripartite lines. The few authorities that tried to pursue comprehensive policies faced very great difficulties; for example, the LCC attempted the impossible and tried to develop comprehensive schools and at the same time preserve some grammar schools. It would be wrong, however, to give the impression that there was at this time a simple contest between the tripartite system and a clear-cut comprehensive policy. Then, as now, there was no clear idea of what a comprehensive school should be. Olive Banks suggests that most of the advocates of common schools at this time had in mind multilateral or multibias schools, which would facilitate transfer from one 'side' to another within the same school rather than schools where all pupils would pursue some kind of common curriculum even for a few years. This is certainly borne out by what happened when the tripartite system gradually became discredited and gave way to a more general nationwide policy of comprehensive schools.

The tripartite system was felt by many to be quite equitable so long as there was parity of esteem between the three types of schools. But this was always an impossibility in our kind of society:

> The Spens and Norwood Committees envisaged three types of secondary education catering for three occupational levels and three types of ability and aptitude, yet enjoying parity of esteem in the eyes of parents, pupils and teachers. If, however, the prestige of a school derives from the social and economic status of the occupations for which it prepares, then equality of prestige is clearly impossible between the non-selective modern schools and the selected grammar schools (Banks, 1955: 242-43).

Children who were selected for grammar schools were labelled as successes; the others were necessarily failures, however good the school might be in purely educational terms. The move away from the tripartite system was thus encouraged not so much by the conviction that comprehensive schools were 'right' but that the 11+ examination for selection at an early age was somehow 'wrong'.

The comprehensive schools which began to develop in the 1950s and 1960s were in the main tripartite systems under one roof. They were encouraged to 'stream like mad' (Pedley, 1969: 98). Pedley in the same book also suggests that the Labour Ministers of Education were no match for ministry officials who strongly favoured retaining the grammar schools with quite different curricula from the secondary modern schools. Gradually the focus of educational discussion moved away from the iniquities of 11+ testing to the question of school organization — particularly the question of streaming. Julienne Ford (1969) showed that the criticisms which had been levelled against the tripartite system also applied to streamed comprehensive schools. If middle-class children were at an advantage in getting access to and achieving academic results within grammar schools, then more or less the same process was at work in streamed comprehensive schools: working-class children were over-represented in the lower streams, had poorer academic records, and left school earlier than middle-class pupils of the same measured intelligence.

In 1957 the British Pyschological Society published the results of an enquiry into *Secondary School Selection* edited by P. E. Vernon. The report did not condemn selection or streaming as such but expressed very clear worries about the 'stereotyping effects of streaming by ability':

> In the light of these findings the dangers of streaming are obvious. Children who are relegated to a low stream, to suite their present level of ability, are likely to be taught at a slower pace; whereas the brighter streams, often under the better teachers, are encouraged to proceed more rapidly. Thus initial differences become exacerbated, and those duller children who happen to improve later fall too far behind the higher streams in attainment to be able to catch up, and lose the chance to show their true merits . . . . This stereotyping effect is particularly serious, also, at the secondary stage where the modern school curriculum naturally falls more and more behind that of the grammar school. Unpublished research by Vernon has shown that, after three years in the modern school, pupils are more re-tarded relative to grammar school pupils than when they entered — not because they have learned nothing but because with lesser

pressure of examinations, homework, etc., they have not continued to learn as rapidly as have grammar pupils. Not only attainment test scores but also intelligence quotients, show this tendency to diverge as a result of streaming (Vernon, 1955; Daniels, 1955). (From Vernon, 1957: 42-43.)

Hargreaves (1967) also described the very disturbing unintended consequences resulting from secondary school streaming. He showed that there existed in the secondary modern school he studied two opposed sub-cultures — the academic high streams and the 'delinquescent' low streams. All of this provided negative evidence against the tripartite system and streaming. But this has been one of the general weaknesses of the anti-tripartite position. An egalitarian view of education is clearly against grammar schools, against selection, against streaming. But what is it for? What does social justice in education really mean?

In 1969 Marten Shipman wrote a paper for the British Sociological Association which showed that even a comprehensive school which avoided rigid segregation of pupils might still produce and perpetuate gross inequalities:

The consequences of reforms in education have often disappointed the reformers and distorted their intentions. As the rate of social change increases and the schools come under greater pressure to accept innovations, the importance of trying to anticipate these unintended consequences increases. Sociologists particularly have been active, not only in showing that the emerging school system favoured children from middle class homes, but in pressing for de-streaming and comprehensive education as steps to remedy the inequality. Yet it is difficult to view new forms of school organisation with optimism. Furthermore, it may be that this drive for a fairer school system is being counteracted by contemporary curriculum developments. Both movements are being promoted by reformers anxious to improve the quality of education for all, but they may be cancelling each other out, or even producing a greater divide than ever between the education of the elite and the majority. (Shipman in Hooper, 1971: 101.)

John White (1968) tackling the question of comprehensive school curricula from a philosophical point of view came to broadly similar conclusions, except that he put more of the blame on the Schools Council which, he alleged, had devoted too much of its resources to developing curricula for 'young school leavers' or the supposed 'less able pupils'. The Schools Council had intentionally or unintentionally encouraged comprehensive schools to think in terms of different kinds of curriculum for different leves of pupil or different kinds of ability.

Perhaps the most common hidden device for compartmentalizing and segregating curricula and pupils is the widespread use of 'options'. In most comprehensive schools today pupils at the end of the third year (that is about the age of 14) are invited to construct their own fourth or fifth year programme by selecting from lists of options. These lists may vary in complexity and in some schools choice is greater than in others but they have a good deal in common. Although the options scheme is usually justified in terms of pupil choice, real choice is much more doubtful and the system often becomes manipulation rather than real freedom to choose. Real choice is often very limited: there is no guarantee of the chosen options being available for all pupils, pupils often choose (or fail to choose) without knowing exactly what they are choosing, teachers are selected rather than the subjects, and so on. There is a long list of objections to the options scheme upon which it would be inappropriate to elaborate now, but two of them are of particular importance in our argument. First, option choices plus a system of counselling often becomes a disguised form of streaming; this is similar in effect to what often happens to working-class pupils in the US under the heading of 'cooling out'; secondly, the chosen options may result in a very unbalanced or inadequate curriculum. For example, far too many boys (and even more girls) give up mathematics and science; far too many pupils find that having neglected to choose a certain option at age 14 they are then very much limited in their choice of career at 16, 18 or much later. In schools where streaming and setting have been curtailed it is most important to avoid curriculum segregation under the guise of choice or options. It is all the more important to counter this trend since it is often couched in 'progressive' terms such as 'following children's interests' or the importance of freedom in education — a topic to which we shall have to return in later chapters.

The history of secondary education in the twentieth century might be summarized in the following way, being an account of a gradual move away from the idea of intellectual segregation.

(1) At the beginning of the century secondary education was for a minority: some were selected because they could pay, some because they were very clever. This was an interesting mixture of social elitism and intellectual elitism.

(2) Egalitarian pressures throughout the 1920s and 1930s brought about 'secondary education for all' in 1944 but this was generally interpreted as two or three different kinds of school: the tripartite system plus parity of prestige. This was officially moving into a 'pure' system of *intellectual* segregation but there were still clear overtones of social elitism in the system.

(3) Selection proved to be difficult to administer 'fairly', and parity of prestige was clearly not operating, so selective schools gradually gave way to comprehensive schools which were — in the 1950s — mostly selective systems under one roof.

(4) As evidence concerning the disadvantages of streaming built up, together with teachers' experience, there was a move to setting rather than rigid streaming, and mixed ability experiments, at first in the lower forms, later for a wider age range.

(5) In the 1970s there was wider discussion of the idea of a common curriculum, based on the argument that there was little point in having a common school unless it was transmitting some kind of common culture by means of a common curriculum.

It would be very nice to be able to end the story at this point and suggest that all that is necessary now is to allow schools a little time to work out exactly what the common curriculum should be and how to organize it for efficient teaching for all levels of ability. Unfortunately there are at least two complications. First, the pattern of development or movement away from segregation in secondary schools is by no means as neat as my five stages might suggest: some LEAs are still fighting a rear-guard action against moving from stage 2 to stage 3; many schools have stuck at stage 3; most are probably at stage 4 (see Benn and Simon, 1970). The battle against segregation has been won at the level of research evidence and enlightened experience, but this cannot convince those who simply refuse to believe that segregation by intellectual type is not an essential aspect of good secondary organization.

The second complication is at the level of research. I have tried to show in this chapter, briefly and probably inadequately, that the psychological research on intelligence could not possibly support the view that there are different *types* of children requiring different kinds of education. In other words, intelligence was a question of more or less rather than categorizing into types, and that it has proved to be impossible to draw a line anywhere (for example, at the

IQ of 120) and say above that line are the academic pupils
and below that they are non-academic. However good the
test there is always a very big grey area. Moreover, despite the
probable existence of something called 'general intelligence',
most people are much more academic in some fields than in
others. It is very dangerous and very harmful to label children
at the age of 11, or even later, as academic or non-academic
or as grammar types and secondary modern types.

This was generally accepted by psychologists in the 1950s
and 1960s, especially when cultural differences in test per-
formances were carefully examined by psychologists.

> Current notions of intelligence have changed tremendously . . . over
> the past half century or so. We realise that mental abilities are much
> too varied to be adequately described in terms of a monolithic
> general intelligence or Spearman's G-factor. There are many more
> specialised types of ability — verbal, numerical, spacial and per-
> ceptual, memorising, reasoning, mechanical, imaginative and so on,
> and the same individual may well be quite high in one, low in
> another, although on the whole they tend to correlate positively
> (Vernon, 1969: 21).

But there are two interconnected developments which have
taken place in educational research which might be used to
attack my plea for a common curriculum. The first is the
failure of many of the American compensatory education
programmes; the second is the revival of the idea of two
kinds of intelligence in the work of Arthur Jensen.

The failure of compensatory education might be thought
to be relevant for this reason. In America (and to some
extent in the UK) the attack on inequality in education has
taken the form of an extreme environmentalist position on
the nature of intelligence. This argument is, roughly, that IQ
is entirely or very largely determined by environment, and
that if you catch the child early enough, improve his educa-

tional environment, you can raise his IQ and therefore his later educational chances. (I would like to stress that this is not a point of view that I have ever adopted.) The results generally have been disappointing — at least in terms of IQ improvement. But this does not affect the argument I have been putting forward about a common curriculum. The point I wish to make is not that all children are potentially more or less the same, but that all 'normal' children share certain educational rights — rights of access to worthwhile knowledge and experiences. I object to the idea that only a few can benefit from real education and the rest should be fobbed off with socialization for conformity and learning a few useful skills. The problem is not how to raise a child's IQ from 90 to 95, but how to give a below-average pupil access to a worthwhile curriculum. In my view the American compensatory education programmes havebeen wrongly designed, in over-emphasising the possibility of raising IQ.

The second development, Jensen's research, is potentially more dangerous, not for what it actually demonstrates but because the case might be distorted and over-simplified, and has been on several occasions. Jensen (1969) in an interesting article in the *Harvard Educational Review* began by asking the question I have already suggested is not relevant to the question of a common curriculum: 'How much can we boost IQ and scholastic achievement?' He was particularly concerned with the US problem of negro children's under-achievement in schools and the failure of compensatory education programmes to boost IQ. The assumption had been made that it should have been possible to boost the IQ of negroes because they tended to perform less well on conventional IQ tests than white children. Jensen's research suggested that the other possibility should not be ignored: namely, that negro children were, on average, less intelligent. Jensen suggested that it might be more productive therefore

to switch funds away from attempts to boost IQ to research
proposals for finding more effective methods of teaching.
Jensen then went further and claimed that he had identified
two kinds of ability: 'associative learning ability' and 'conceptual learning ability'; whereas negro children tended to
fall behind the whites on conceptual learning ability (more
abstract learning tasks), he found no significant differences in
associative learning ability (auditory digit memory, serial
ordering, learning to associate pairs of pictures, recalling
names, etc.).

This research might be dangerous if misunderstood or
over-simplified. In the hands of an American racist, for
example, such research might be used to resist the desegregation of schools on the basis of colour. The argument might
go something like this:

(1) negroes are less intelligent than whites;
(2) they have a different way of thinking; therefore
(3) keep them in separate schools.

By extension you might then apply the same argument to
academic and non-academic children in the UK (or, like
Bantock, to working-class and middle-class children in the
UK). But this simply will not do (and of course this was not
the conclusion reached by Jensen himself). Jensen claims
(and the experts are still arguing about this issue) that the
distribution of intelligence is different for blacks and whites:
but there is an enormous overlap. The figures produced could
never be used to support segregated schools. Secondly,
Jensen does not say that whites have one kind of intelligence
(conceptual learning ability) and blacks have only associative
learning ability, both groups have both kinds of ability, but,
he suggests, blacks perform better on associative learning
ability than they do on conceptual learning ability. His conclusion is that teaching methods should make use of the
strengths of the pupils rather than their weaknesses and that

those teaching black children should bear in mind the research evidence on the differences that have been found. As I understand the Jensen position, it is for developing new approaches in teaching methods, *not* a proposal for a different kind of curriculum.

Both kinds of research, therefore, seem to me to be irrelevant to the notion of the common curriculum, but to be extremely important in stressing the need for recognizing varieties of learning styles in children and therefore for developing a variety of teaching methods in mixed ability classes. A useful analogy might be made here to the field of nutrition. The nutritionists who identified what all human beings need to eat in order to survive — vitamins, proteins, etc. — have not suggested that we should all eat exactly the same meals three times a day. Similarly, the proposal that *all* children, whatever their abilities and tastes, need a certain kind of curriculum diet to meet their basic needs in surviving in our kind of society, does not mean that everyone will have the same kind of curriculum for the whole length of their schooling. Individual tastes and individual abilities need to be catered for as well. In England, however, the tendency in the twentieth century (but not in the nineteenth) has been to stress variety and to ignore the problem of a basic curriculum diet. We now need to specify the equivalent of vitamins, carbohydrates and proteins as a basis for a common core curriculum. But we should also recognize that the curriculum problem is much more complex than nutrition. Solving this problem is not helped by those who deny the existence of differences altogether, nor by those — the intellectual elitists — who over-simplify the differences into a few basic types and ignore children's common educational needs.

4

NAIVE PROGRESSIVISM

It is unfortunate that certain standpoints in education have been labelled as 'progressive' and have then become identified with other reformist views which have very little if anything in common with them. This is certainly the case with the kind of extreme child-centred attitudes which are associated with the doctrine that the freedom of the individual child to develop unimpeded by society is the supreme goal of education. The main assumption behind this point of view is that the child knows best what is good for him (physically and educationally) so that he should be allowed complete freedom to decide what activities to get involved in at any particular time. In support of this dogma a comparison is often made by some 'progressive' educationists between a child choosing food and choosing educational or other activities. They quote the well-known experiment which allowed children in early infancy to choose their own food from a very wide range of choice and then measured what had been taken, and it was established that all children had chosen a well-balanced diet. (It is often not pointed out that when the young children were offered the wide range of food to choose from certain kinds of temptations such as cakes and chocolate were excluded from the range of choice.)

The earliest well-known exponent of this point of view is Jean Jacques Rousseau (1712-78) although even his pronouncements are so ambiguous that it would be difficult to take them as a justification for some of the extreme child-centred practices which have been adopted more recently. In many respects Rousseau's ideas — or at least some of them — have dominated progressive education ever since the end of the eighteenth century. But in many other respects Rousseau could be seen as simply reacting against the current 'heaven-centred' philosophy of his time by demanding happiness now rather than in a doubtful heaven at some time in the future. Rousseau's basic view was that man is naturally good but may be and usually is, corrupted by his social institutions: 'Let us lay it down as an incontravertible rule that the first impulses of nature are always right; there is no original sin in the human heart . . .' (Rousseau, 1911: 56).

Children were seen not simply as miniature adults as was usually the case in his day but as individuals passing through stages which were important in their own right, not merely as a harsh preparation for a difficult adult life to come:

> Nature would have them children before they are men. If we try to invert this order we shall produce a forced fruit immature and flavourless, a fruit which will be rotten before it is ripe; we shall have young doctors and old children. Childhood has its own ways of thinking, seeing and feeling; nothing is more foolish than to try and substitute our ways; and I should no more expect judgment in a ten year old child than I should expect him to be five feet high (p. 54).

There are two difficulties here: one is that we might very well now admit that Rousseau had a point in saying that childhood activities should be respected for their own sake, and that education should take account of them, but that does not necessarily rule out the possibility that another function of education is to prepare children for some aspects of adult life as well as letting them enjoy their own childhood. A second difficulty is the extreme way in which this view is expressed; for example, that a ten-year-old child is not expected to have any kind of judgement. The same is true about the interaction between children and their society. Rousseau was quite clear that education should not teach children to fit into society in any respect, but the aim should be to allow children to be free from the shackles of society.

Here again there is scope for misinterpretation of Rousseau's point even if we are sufficiently charitable to believe that Rousseau was clear about what he was saying. It does appear that Rousseau suggested that in a good society which followed the 'general will' an adult would obey the rules of society, but this would be obedience to his own rational self as expressed in the laws. Adults would thus be both social *and* free in the ideal society. One task of education was to avoid premature, 'irrational' obedience in children. It is never quite clear whether we should blame Rousseau or his more extreme followers for the doctrine that children should be allowed to do anything that they wish to do — all in the name of education. Rousseau was equally condemnatory about some aspects of the education of his day:

> Man's proper study is that of his relationship to his environment so long as he knows that environment through his physical nature, he should study himself in relation to things; this is the business of his childhood; when he begins to be aware of his moral nature, he should study himself in relation to his fellow men (p. 175).

Rousseau also had much to say about how children should learn, again providing slogans for the child-centred educationists ever since:

> A man must know many things which seem useless to a child, but

need the child learn, or indeed can he learn, all that the man must know? Try to teach the child what is of use to a child and you will find that it takes all his time. Why urge him to the studies of an age he may never reach, to the neglect of those studies which meet his present needs. 'But', you ask 'would it not be too late to learn what he ought to know when the time comes to use it?' I cannot tell; but this I do know, it is impossible to teach it sooner, for our real teachers are experience and emotion, and man will never learn what befits a man except under its own conditions (p. 175).

In many respects Rousseau was simply reacting against the harsh traditional attitudes towards children typical of his day. The kind of view of education which has been described by A. A. Evans as the classical-Christian tradition which assumed that children were naturally evil, and that the main value of learning was moral and intellectual training for adult life. But it would be very strange if we simply accepted Rousseau's views without looking carefully at the assumptions behind them and at any empirical evidence which might support Rousseau or contradict him. Unfortunately many of the extreme child-centred advocates put forward the views of the naturally good child and the completely evil society as an unquestioned and unquestionable doctrine.

Brian Simon in *History of Education 1780 to 1870* has described how Rousseau's works were very popular and influential among the educational radicals of the eighteenth and early nineteenth centuries. Simon also shows how disenchantment often set in when Rousseau's methods were actually put to the test:

So impressed was Edgeworth with the Rousseau system by contrast with the 'obvious deficiencies and absurdities . . . in the treatment of children in almost every family' with which he was acquainted, that he determined to leave 'the body and mind of my son . . . as much as possible to the education of nature and of accident'. In this course he continued for five years until the child was eight years old when on a visit to Paris he introduced him to Rousseau, who took the boy for a walk and pronounced himself in general satisfied with his development. From Paris Edgeworth proceeded to Lyons where, characteristically, he applied all his energy to a scheme for turning the course of the Rhone, leaving the supervision of his son's education to Thomas Day who took on the task with enthusiasm.

Not long afterwards however Edgeworth abandoned the experiment. The boy had developed considerable abilities, he recalled later in his memoirs:

> 'Uncommon strength and hardiness of body, great vivacity, and was not a little disposed to think and act for himself .,. . whatever regarded the health, strength, and agility of my son, had amply justified the system of my master; but I found myself entangled in difficulties with regard to my child's mind and temper. He was generous, brave, good-natured, and what is commonly called good tempered; but he was scarcely to be controlled. It was difficult to urge him to anything that did not suit his fancy, and more difficult to restrain him from what he wished to follow. In short, he was self-willed, from a spirit of independence which had been inculcated by his early education, and which he cherished the more from the inexperience of his own powers' (Edgeworth Memoirs, Vol. I, pp. 268-69).

Edgeworth therefore rejected Rousseau's conception of natural virtue, and, though continuing to consider the child's needs, stressed in his writings the importance of forming human and moral qualities. (Simon, 1960: 39-40).

Such accounts as this are rarely mentioned by the progressives who quote Rousseau with such affection and treat him as an accepted authority on education. In some Colleges of Education Rousseau's *Emile* has been prescribed as a set book to be studied and cherished. It is a great pity that a more critical attitude has not been taken to such extreme

views. Rousseau is a very interesting and important writer but
he should be regarded as someone to be studied in the
context of eighteenth-century social change, not as an
authority for all time.

Pestalozzi (1746-1827) should be seen in much the same
light, although he was a more respectable educationist than
Rousseau. Even so, he too should be seen in the historical
and social context of Europe at the end of the eighteenth
century rather than someone who has a message for all time.
The key to Pestalozzi's educational doctrine is partly his own
personal history. He was born into a privileged family in
Zurich, but when he was 6 his father died and the family
experienced some hardship. Concern for the poor and the
under-privileged — even if sometimes in a paternalistic way —
was one of the dominant features of Pestalozzi's life:

> The poor must be educated for poverty and this is the key test by
> which it can be discovered whether such an institution is really a
> good one. Education of the poor demands a deep and accurate
> knowledge of the real needs, limitations and environment of
> poverty, and detailed knowledge of the probable situation in which
> they will spend their lives . . .. (Quoted in *Pestalozzi* by M. R.
> Heafford, 1967: 9-10.)

As a young man, before the French Revolution, Pestalozzi
was a member of a group calling themselves 'The Patriots'
who demanded radical political and social reform. During this
period of his life he read Rousseau's *Emile* (1762), and
although he described it as a 'highly impractical dream book'
he was influenced by it — particularly by the idea of stages of
development and Rousseau's view of natural education. But
after the Revolution Pestalozzi's views tended to become
more conservative and he increasingly saw education as a
means of avoiding social conflict.

Like Rousseau, Pestalozzi firmly believed that the child was born good but was in constant danger of being corrupted or damaged by society. As well as accepting the validity of 'innate goodness', Pestalozzi developed Rousseau's idea of the child's world being significantly different from that of the adult. Reacting against what he saw as the unnatural cruelty and harshness of eighteenth-century schools, Pestalozzi, who believed in a completely benevolent Nature, felt that a teacher should care for each pupil and protect him from the evils of society just as Nature looks after plants:

> Man, imitate the action of great Nature which from the seed of even the largest tree pushes at first but an imperceptible shoot, but then by a further imperceptible growth which progresses smoothly every hour and every day unfolds the young trunk, then that which will grow into the main branches . . . (p. 44).

We should recognize that there was great value in ideas such as these as a counter-balance to the very unsatisfactory shools of the eighteenth and early nineteenth centuries. But Pestalozzi, like Rousseau, was guilty of two major errors. The first was that he made a false analogy between a growing plant and a growing child; secondly, both Pestalozzi and Rousseau failed to see that it was necessary for a child to interact with his own society. To assume that all aspects of society are automatically bad and that all aspects of human nature are entirely good is naive in the extreme. It is this naivety which has caused so much harm in later nineteenth and twentieth-century educational discussion.

The third great hero of the naive progressivists is Friedrich Froebel (1782-1852). The dominant influences on Froebel's educational ideas were German idealist philosophy and his own reflections on Christian theology. It has been said that these two influences were never reconciled in what emerged as his own philosophy of education.

Froebel's approach to education is a religious one, and his religion, in spirit and in language, is Christian. His opportunity to teach seemed to him in retrospect a religious vocation, and the circumstances in which it came to show the working of a 'Good Providence'. It is not possible to discuss his philosophy of education without conceding that in his own mind its source and its vindication came from his religious belief. He affirms it explicitly and vigorously in his definitions of purpose and his descriptions of method. He implies it consistently as he describes the field of educational activity.

> Education as a whole . . . will bring to man's consciousness and render efficient in his life the fact that man and nature proceed from God and are conditioned by Him — that both have their being in God . . . therefore the school should first of all teach the religion of Christ; therefore it should first of all, and above all, give instruction in the Christian religion; everywhere and in all zones the school should instruct for and in this religion. (H. A. Hamilton, 'The Religious Roots of Froebel's Philosophy', in E. Lawrence (ed.), *Friedrich Froebel and English Education*, 1952, p. 166.)

Hamilton, a generally sympathetic reviewer of Froebel's work, is critical of the inadequate basis of his educational theory:

> Froebel would seem to be selective and partial in his conception of nature. His approach is that of a man who has learned how to contemplate but has chosen to look only at what he wanted to see. There is no suspicion even of nature's indifference to man's welfare: no hint of nature as being a cause of suffering in man, both in body and in mind. . . . The approach is that of a contemplative artist not the scientist or even the theologian (p. 170).

Froebel, like Rousseau and Pestalozzi, was dominated by the idea of in-born goodness:

> My teachers are the children themselves with their purity and inno-

cence, their unconsciousness, and their irresistible claims, and I follow them like a faithful, trustful scholar (p. 23).

Froebel's view of the child was that he was pure and innocent and also an expression of divinity: even to suggest that the child might be morally neutral rather than completely good was blasphemous: 'Every human being should be viewed and treated as a manifestation of the divine spirit in human form' (p. 174). Froebel therefore condemned contemporary views which suggested that the child was a lump of clay or wax to be moulded. Another generally sympathetic writer on Froebel, Nathan Isaacs, is also critical of the inadequacy of Froebel's theory:

If we turn . . . to Froebel's actual picture of the child, I think we may say, in the light of our more modern knowledge, that it is far too simple on the one hand and far too idealised on the other (p. 201).

Froebel, like Rousseau and Pestalozzi, may have had a generally beneficial effect in countering the harshness of nineteenth-century schools, but he also has much to answer for. The extreme naivety of Froebel's views has been intensified rather than diminished in the writings of his followers. It is arguable that the metaphor of the kindergarten is one of the most misleading in the whole of educational thought. The idea that a gardener allows plants to grow and merely stands back and watches them has been used as an excuse for all sorts of chaos and neglect in many classrooms.

Rousseau, Pestalozzi and Froebel are the three great authorities most often used to justify the practices of the naive progressivists. Dewey's writings have also been used by progressives of various shades but, fortunately, although he supported progressive education for many years and did much to spread a more enlightened approach to education all over the world, he lived long enough to dissociate himself publicly from the Progressive Education Association, and spent a good deal of his energy in the latter part of his life trying to correct the extravagances of progressive education, especially in the US (M. S. Dworkin, 1959, Editor's Note, p. 113).

There have, of course, also been numerous twentieth-century prophets of 'freedom in education' and other pro-gressivist slogans. I will mention just two of them: the American Homer Lane and the Scot, A. S. Neill. Homer Lane was born in New England in 1876 into a working-class, strict Baptist family. He ran away from home at age 14 and experienced a number of manual jobs before becoming a grocery clerk and getting married at age 22. When he became a father he was so fascinated by the process of child rearing that he decided to train to become a teacher. He studied at the Sloyd Training School in Boston and had a good deal of experience, including teaching prison convicts as well as children in normal schools. He gained a good deal of very varied experience by the age of 30 when he became the Superintendent of a Boys' Home. Lane's main contribution was his attempt to introduce self-government. He found a number of official constraints to his ideas in the US, so he visited England in 1911 on a lecture tour. While he was here he became involved in plans for a reformatory school in Dorset which began in 1912 as 'The Little Commonwealth'. Lane achieved remarkable results in The Little Common-wealth until it was closed down in 1918 after some un-fortunate publicity. In so far as Lane had a theory it was that the main cause of delinquency was in 'the repression of *élan vital*'. His methods at the Commonwealth were to encourage freedom and responsibility among the delinquent boys. Some of his practices may have been considered excessive; for example, actively destroying his own authority by joining in gang activities and even inciting them to further destruction. Some of his writing suggests that he admitted their destructive impulses, and that he felt that such views about property were just as valid as the protective morality of the more prosperous middle classes. Apart from these excesses there were two flaws in applying Homer Lane's views about the Little Commonwealth to education generally. The first was that Homer Lane's experiment was essentially concerned with the treatment of disturbed delinquent boys (even if he sometimes doubted whether they were really disturbed or not). Education certainly took second place or even third place to the main purposes of the Little Commonwealth. As with many so-called progressives in education Homer Lane was much more interested in child-rearing and putting right what had gone wrong with child rearing at an earlier stage than with education itself. Lane and most of the others in the progressive movement had almost nothing to say about the content of the curriculum apart from negative remarks. The second fallacy in trying to apply Homer Lane's methods to normal educational processes is that, whether we approve or disapprove of what he was doing, Homer Lane was certainly a very dynamic character. His influence over the delinquent boys was of a personal kind which made it very difficult to generalize his methods. This again is a common fallacy in the literature on progressive schools, namely that because one dynamic figure can work near-miracles with a small group of children using very unorthodox methods that ordinary teachers can achieve similar results with much larger groups of children in normal schools, even though they lack the personal qualities of the original innovator.

A. S. Neill drew his inspiration partly from Homer Lane and tried to apply some of these methods to normal children's education. He was also influenced by the writings of psycho-analysts, especially Freud and Jung; but many psychologists have felt that he misinterpreted and misused the psychological and psycho-analytical theories of the day to bolster up his own anti-authority attitudes. It may be no coincidence that Neill also had a very strict up-bringing. Neill's father, George Neill, was the school master in the village school of Kingsmuir where A. S. Neill eventually went to school. At home and at school George Neill was apparently a very firm disciplinarian, wielding the Scottish tawse as part of the natural way of preserving discipline. It would not seem far-fetched to suggest that a good deal of Neill's attitudes to authority are connected with his rebellion against the values and standards of his parents. It sometimes appears in his writings that Neill was really much more concerned with justifying his own behaviour by any kind of theory that he could invent or adopt second-hand.

It was not just parental authority that he rejected but the whole idea of a cultural heritage. For example, he often made such remarks as 'To write a bad limerick is better than to learn *Paradise Lost* by heart' (*The Problem Child*, p. 178). Whether he meant this to be taken literally or not may be questioned, but the important fact is that his educational practices and those of his followers have appeared to support such a statement. In other words naive progressivists attach a very high value to children's self-expression and a very low value to appreciating the highly regarded self-expression of others. The problem of taste and standards and the real meaning of the value of literature is ignored in Neill's writings.

Neill had a good deal of experience in this country and abroad before setting up his own school, Summerhill. Although many of these schools were regarded as extremely progressive, none of them was progressive enough for Neill. In all of them he found that he wanted to give children much more freedom than even the most progressive establishment was prepared to tolerate. Neill's real value is in taking the belief in children's goodness and children's freedom to the extreme: so much so that it is sometimes difficult to see why he regarded it necessary to have schools or teachers at all.

> So he would expel authority: 'Obedience is tolerable only when it is a mutual contract'. Punishment certainly must go; 'It deals with results, not causes.' Respect too is not an attribute for the teacher to cultivate, because it contains fear. 'The only way to teach is to love . . . read Froebel, Montesorri, Freud, Jung; read and re-read the life of Jesus Christ.' But no moralising. 'Shall I teach my children the difference between right and wrong?' asks the young teacher. 'No', I reply, for you do not know the difference between right and wrong'. 'I do!' she protests indignantly. And I answer 'Suppose you know what is right and wrong for you; do you know what is right and wrong for your child?' (Hemmings, 1972: 35).

Neill's disregard for the curriculum is illustrated by his attitude to the teaching arrangements at one of the schools he was involved in before settling down to Summerhill. At Hellerau in Germany, Neill opened up a new school in co-operation with Frau Baer.

> They began to plan and dream 'of a school where creation will be the chief object, where the child will do rather than learn, where he will make his own books rather than reading lesson books, where he will spend a month making a ship if he wants to'. They would provide three channels — art, crafts and eurhythmics — along one of which each child would choose to go from the age of about 14. A fourth channel — science — they had to reject because it would have been too expensive to cater for properly (Hemmings, 1972: 45).

This planning of a curriculum was even then very half-hearted, and in his later experiments Neill was even less conscious of the need to be concerned about the content of children's educational programmes. Neill appeared to have no kind of theory about what modern philosophers of education might call worthwhile knowledge and worthwhile activities in education. The only criterion of worthwhileness which appeared to be relevant to him was whether it interested the children or not. The teacher had no role to play in guiding children towards activities which he felt might be more worthwhile. 'No man is good enough to tell another how to live. No man is wise enough to guide another's footsteps' (*The Problem Child*, p. 217).

> So long as Jimmy is interfering with the freedom of others the crowd is within its rights to restrain him, but it would have no right to influence, for instance, Jimmy's decision as whether he should go to lessons. That is entirely his affair, and however he chooses he will not be infringing the liberty of others. To compel a child to learn Latin was on a par with forcing a man to adopt a religion by Act of Parliament, Neill thought. And he added that it was equally foolish, because the child would learn much more efficiently through his own volitions than as a result of compulsion. However, Neill was not proposing some subtle form of manipulation. It was the child's right of decision that was his passionate concern, and he was genuinely unworried as to whether or not his pupils learnt Latin — or anything else, for that matter. They would learn something because they were human beings, but precisely what they learnt did not matter and did not have to be prescribed (Hemmings, 1972: 73).

This was the view expressed by someone who generally admired Neill and was a teacher in Summerhill for many years.

Another doctrine which Lane and Neill shared was the idea of innate goodness or 'original virtue'. It is very difficult to know what this means apart from being a rejection of the idea of original sin or the need to punish children in order to make them good. If this is all that was meant then undoubtedly both Lane and Neill made a contribution to twentieth-century humanity, if not to education, by rejecting the idea that children needed punishment to counteract their evil. But if original virtue is intended to be the basis of any kind of educational theory then it is very difficult to understand exactly what can be meant by this. It is particularly difficult to know what both Lane and Neill meant by original goodness since they both elsewhere appear to reject the idea of goodness in any absolute sense. They were relativists morally and culturally. One possible interpretation of original goodness is that Lane and Neill meant that anything 'instinctive' is good, and any attempt to restrain 'natural' impulses is automatically bad. This now seems a very naive view of human nature, and can only be given any credit at all as a necessary counter-blast to nineteenth-century ideas of natural evil. But it appeared to be necessary for Lane and Neill to reject neutrality and to insist on original goodness. If human nature was neutral and therefore capable of becoming either good or evil then it would not have been sensible to have adopted the policy of letting children develop *without* adult intervention. The only excuse for allowing children to do what they want to do was the assumption that what was natural was good and any intervention was unnatural and therefore bad. In retrospect this seems a very foolish doctrine and not one that was shared by most other progressive educationists of the day.

Other pioneers in the New Education Movement reached different conclusions about innate goodness. For example, Bertrand Russell, although sympathetic to some of Neill's ideas, found himself at odds with Neill on this particular issue. Despite obvious differences Neill wanted to claim Russell as an ally when he and his wife Dora Russell opened Beacon Hill School in 1927. Neill declared that this was the only school in England besides Summerhill that was 'demonstrating complete freedom in choice of work and behaviour' (*The Problem Parent,* p. 107). But Russell's views as expressed in his book *On Education* were quite different from Neill's. Russell, whilst rejecting the Christian idea of original sin, also rejected the opposite error 'that is the belief that children are naturally virtuous'. Russell's view was that they were 'born only with reflexes and a few instincts. Out of these, by action of the environment, habits are produced which may be either healthy or morbid' (Russell, 1926: 24). At this time Russell was much more sympathetic to the psychological view than to the Psycho-analytic writings of which Neill was so fond. Russell clearly felt that there were certain qualities which children ought to be encouraged to acquire: vitality, sensitiveness, intelligence and courage, for example. Just as it was a parent's responsibility to encourage the development of these virtues in children so teachers should also be interested in the development of these good habits. At this stage Russell felt that behaviourist psychology had something to offer in helping teachers to foster these virtues. On this point Neill was completely opposed to the Russell view, and yet he ignored all this and claimed Russell as an ally. Even on the question of freedom, although both men valued freedom very highly, they did so for quite different reasons. For Russell freedom was important because it was a way of learning more efficiently. But for Neill we constantly get the impression that freedom was the *only* consideration — he appeared to be almost completely uninterested in whether they learnt anything else or not. Unlike Russell, Neill had little or no respect for the traditional culture. He was unconcerned if children left his school completely ignorant of science, mathematics, literature or the arts, as long as they had expressed themselves in some way. Russell's attitude to authority was also quite different from Neill's. Russell wrote: 'Those who educate have to find a way of exercising authority in accordance with the spirit of liberty' (Russell, 1916: 102). Russell's solution was that a teacher must have a certain respect for children and be conscious of the problem of authority and have reverence or 'an unaccountable humility' which would make him ask when it was necessary to bring authority to bear by limiting the freedom of children rather than the traditional teacher's attitude of approaching the problem by putting authority in the first place and then allowing children a certain amount of freedom so long as it did not threaten the teacher's authority. This was a very radical departure from current pedagogical methods that Russell was offering, but even so it was quite different in principle and in practice from what Neill was putting into operation at Summerhill. It is difficult to know whether Neill was aware of the magnitude of the gap between himself and Russell, but it is clear that Russell was aware of their differences. When he wrote to H. G. Wells asking for financial assistance for Beacon Hill School he referred to this difference in his attitude to intellectual development and that of Neill. 'You will realise that hardly any other educational reformers lay much stress upon intelligence. A. S. Neill for example, who is in many ways an admirable man, allows such complete liberty that his children fail to get the necessary training and are always going to the cinema, when they might otherwise be interested in things of more value' (Russell, 1968: 181). For Russell this was probably the greatest of Neill's deficiencies. For those who followed Neill's advice it has probably been the most dangerous part of his doctrine.

I have taken a good deal of space in discussing A. S. Neill because he is one example of a recent advocate of extreme child-centred approaches in education who has actually put his methods into operation in a school situation. But how successful was he? In fact his experience is of very little use in generalizing about child-centred methods or discovery techniques in most other schools. Summerhill was a fee-paying boarding school, catering for the children (often the problem children) of parents who have been referred to as 'middle-class deviants', and without employing any meaningful kind of evaluation. The main attempt to introduce Neill's ideas into a state school − Risinghill − was a conspicuous failure. The success attributed to ex-pupils of Summerhill by Neill himself are clearly exaggerated. The most systematic account of ex-pupils was made by Emmanuel Bernstein (1967; 1968) who interviewed fifty ex-pupils. (The research has been summarized in Hemming (1972).) Bernstein interviewed fifty ex-pupils to assess the affects of their Summerhill experience. Twenty-six of the fifty complained of the lack of academic opportunity and the poor quality of teaching. In particular the role of the teachers was never clear. Neill was an authority of a charismatic kind, but he objected to teachers sharing in this kind of role, and since he had little respect for conventional learning it was difficult to see what the purpose of the teacher was in the school. The suggestion was sometimes made that teachers were there to stoke the boiler and darn the socks (Hemming, 1972: 190). Other criticisms of the school by pupils included the suggestion that the self-expression type of regime favoured the extraverted child but was much less suitable for shy, sensitive introverts. Bernstein's research showed that there were complaints about lack of protection against bullies, insufficient help in academic studies, and the fact that pupils fell into the habit of giving up too easily in the face of difficult work. The limited research that has been carried out did not support Neill's claim that a large proportion of his pupils eventually found work in the arts rather than in more conventional jobs.

It has often been difficult to criticize Neill because of the vagueness of his theory. T. W. Moore maintains that a theory of education must have three components: certain assumptions about the nature of man, especially children; assumptions about the aims or purpose of education; and some kind of theory of knowledge and worthwhileness of knowledge. Neill certainly had no theory of knowledge apart from vague feelings about its lack of importance; he had no real theory of men or children apart from a categoric statement about innate goodness. The generally sympathetic Hemming has this to say about Neill's views of children:

> Neill very rarely talked of the needs of children but would speak rather of their 'wants' or 'interests'. He had no elaborately observed map of child development — only a few broad notions as to the nature of children. Perhaps he recognised only two universal psychological needs of children — the need for play and the need for love. These should be unbounded: the child should 'play and play and play'; adults should always be 'on the child's side', supplying all the love and support that were wanted. For the rest, the children themselves should identify their 'needs' and the adults who cared for them should supply them in such measure as was physically practicable, excepting only where the child's wants conflicted with the obvious conditions for his safety (Hemming, 1972: 175).

Thus, Neill's educational practice depended entirely on the idea of children's innate goodness, their need for play and the overriding aim of education *being* freedom. Given this inadequate theory why has Neill been so influential? Just as Rousseau found a place in the minds of those reformers of the eighteenth century who objected to treating children as delinquent adults, so Neill's extreme views have had an immediate appeal for many of those who objected to the Victorian traditions of elementary and public schools based on fear and punishment, and an almost completely bookish curriculum. Something was obviously wrong with most schools, and Neill was perceptive enough to point out many of these ills. But he was a much better demolitionist than a

rebuilder. He was not only an inadequate theorist, he was a
bad theorist in the limited amount of theorizing that he did,
mainly because he over-simplified very complex issues. He
saw easy answers where others were still worried by the
questions. He was basically an intuitionist, and some of his
intuitions were right but many more were wrong. One intui-
tion he shared with Rousseau related to the joy of discovery,
which was partly right and partly wrong (for both Rousseau
and Neill). Neill and many other naive progressivists share
Rousseau's well-known theory of negative education — that
is, they believed that the best thing teachers could do was to
leave children alone to develop naturally. In particular Rousseau and Neill objected to empty verbalization — everything
should be learnt by discovery and experience rather than by
being told the answers by teachers or books. This kind of
naive progressivism, often dressed up with psychological
jargon as 'discovery learning', has been attacked in very
different ways by both Bantock (1959) and Ausubel (1968).

Bantock is particularly keen to demolish the idea that
children should discover everything for themselves, and that
teachers should avoid telling the child any answers by direct
verbal instruction. He criticizes those teachers who follow
blindly the Rousseau command: 'Give your scholar no verbal
leassons; he should be taught by experience alone.' Bantock
points out that Rousseau badly underestimated the power of
language; Rousseau was under the mistaken belief that words
always had something to which they refer, and that unless
the thing to which the word refers had been 'experienced'
they simply constitute meaningless noises to children.
Bantock insists, correctly in my view, that this is not true.
Children are capable of getting considerable joy out of uses
of words which they cannot understand in the full sense. In
some respects also children can only make discoveries for
themselves when they have the necessary language to put

their learning into some meaningful framework. 'It is no good setting children free in a field and asking them to "experience nature"; they can only experience what they already recognise' (Bantock, 1969: 113). Bantock also criticizes the progressive view of 'discovery methods' as leading to a kind of magpie curriculum and also a structureless context for learning; but it is the failure of the progressives to put language in its proper place in learning which is for Bantock the greatest weakness.

Ausubel (1968) makes a much more systematic attack on the exaggerated views of learning by discovery in a whole chapter (chapter 14) which is so detailed and so closely written that I will not attempt to summarize it here. Ausubel is not, however, completely opposed to discovery learning:

> An all-or-none position regarding use of the discovery method is warranted by neither logic nor evidence. The method itself is very useful for certain pedagogic purposes and in certain educational circumstances. The objectionable aspects of the method are certain unwarranted assumptions, over-stated claims, inadequately tested propositions, and, above all some of the reasons advanced for its efficacy. (pp. 471-72).

What Ausubel is particularly concerned to demolish is what he refers to as 'a sentimental type of Rousseauean mysticism and primitivism'. Ausubel is more inclined to accept some of the discovery methods as appropriate to the early stages of education particularly when children have not passed beyond the concrete operational stage of cognitive development. He accepts that some kinds of learning at this stage are appropriate in a context of guided discovery. But as a child's language develops, and as he proceeds into the formal stage and learning becomes more abstract, then discovery methods become less and less applicable. So for our purposes, as the child progresses through secondary education it is likely that the child-centred approach will be superseded by more effective methods. Even at the earlier stages of learning, however, Ausubel is critical of the kind of acclaim that has been given to discovery methods:

> The crucial points at issue however are not whether learning by discovery enhances learning, retention, and transferability, but whether (a) it does so *sufficiently,* for learners who are capable of learning concepts and principles meaningfully *without it,* to warrant the vastly increased expenditure of time it requires; and (b) in view of this time-cost consideration, the discovery method is a feasible technique for transmitting the substantive content of an intellectual or scientific discipline to cognitively mature students who have already mastered its rudiments and basic vocabulary (p. 473).

Ausubel reviews the research studies in considerable detail and comes to the conclusion:

> (a) That most of the articles most commonly cited in the literature . . . actually report no research findings whatsoever . . . (b) that most of the reasonably well controlled studies report negative findings; and (c) that most studies reporting positive findings either fail to control other significant variables or employ questionable techniques of statistical analysis. Thus, actual examination of the research literature allegedly supportive of learning by discovery reveals that valid evidence of this nature is virtually non-existent (pp. 497-98).

Ausubel also casts a doubt on the whole learning by discovery position from a wider cultural argument quoting Stanley (1949: 455) in support:

> The infant is born into a logically ordered world, abounding in problem solutions accumulated during the long span of mankind's sojourn on earth, and this distilled wisdom, called 'culture', con-

stitutes his chief heritage. Were it wiped away, he would become, in all respects, a wild animal, even less well equipped to cope with nature than are the instinct-aided beasts of the jungle. An individual is sagacious in direct proportion to the facility with which he can acquire and use existing knowledge; for even the most brilliantly endowed person can make but few valuable original discoveries. (Quoted by Ausubel, 1968: 475.)

What all this tends to show is that social justice in education is made much more difficult if we neglect the question of how to ensure, by means of a structured curriculum, access to worthwhile knowledge and experience. The major error of the exaggerated child-centred theory is that it encouraged a view of the child which is unrealistic, and a view of learning which is extremely wasteful in its use of time. For some reason the extreme child-centred educationists, those I have referred to as naive progressivists, seem to be frightened of the idea of structure in education and seem to think that this, together with any kind of verbal instruction, is necessarily authoritarian. This seems now to be complete nonsense and very harmful to the whole cause of progress in education.

5

RELATIVISM IN EDUCATION

There is some overlap between the naive progressivists dealt with in the last chapter and the relativists in education who are the concern of this chapter. For example, A. S. Neill was to some extent a relativist (although as we have shown he was not consistently attached to any particular theoretical school). Part of the William Tyndale School problem was the confusion between education, progressive education and the determination not to impart middle-class values and prejudices. Nevertheless it is necessary to pursue these two misleading kinds of non-theory separately. Whereas in Chapter 4 the main emphasis was on showing why extreme versions of child-centred educational theory are fallacious and harmful to children, in this chapter the intention will be to examine the *content* of education and the kind of attitudes and values which should be the concern of schools but which are often rejected for inadequate theoretical reasons.

There are two strands running through relativist discussions of education and the curriculum, one much more extreme than the other. The first is to suggest that the typical school curriculum (primary or secondary) is a reflection of middle-class values and as such is unsuitable for working-class children, and should be replaced by a working-class curriculum which would be a reflection of working-class culture. We will need to examine this view carefully, particularly questioning the two assumptions: first that the typical school curriculum is in any sense 'middle class', secondly, that there could be a working-class curriculum as 'worthwhile' as the present curriculum or as worthwhile as a reformed common curriculum could be. The second — more extreme — strand is to question the concept 'worthwhile' and suggest that any culture or any sub-culture is just as good as any other, and even more extreme that any experience, any kind of knowledge, is just as valuable (or just as worthless?) as any other knowledge or experience. Both of these views are mistaken; and they are often further confused by being mixed up with valid attacks on the traditional curriculum and on pseudo-concepts such as compensatory education. It will be the purpose of this chapter to try to demonstrate why these views are mistaken and to distinguish these naive views from rational criticisms of the traditional curriculum.

One of the major problems in schools today is the content of education, or the curriculum. One reason that has been put forward to explain the development of schools in our society was that as society became more complex in the process of industrialization and urbanization, the knowledge necessary for understanding society became too complex for transmission by family or peer group. Schools eventually had the explicit task of passing on those kinds of knowledge which were regarded as particularly valuable for possession by the next generation. As society became more complex two familiar problems emerged: first *who* should be educated? And second, *what* should be taught? In England, and in most other societies, education was first thought of as particularly necessary for the future leaders of society — whether they were religious leaders or political leaders. The knowledge which was regarded as valuable for them was the kind of knowledge which would contribute towards their leadership — either by giving them power over their subordinates or by being a badge of rank. Some knowledge started by being 'useful' and 'power-giving' and later became simply a badge of rank. For example, Latin in the Middle Ages was a source of power to priests and a medium of knowledge-acquisition for other professionals and scholars (at a time when Latin was the common language of scholarship throughout Europe and a good deal of knowledge was only available in Latin). Later, however, Latin became unnecessary for these purposes but was still taught in schools. It survived partly because it served to identify those destined for social leadership. By this time it was increasingly suggested that the lower orders in society also needed some kind of education. Some said that all should be able to read so that they could have access to the Bible and spiritual salvation; others wanted a factory work-force which possessed basic skills in reading, writing and counting; later still, when there was the possibility of a one-man one-vote situation, some reformers felt that future voters should be well enough informed to make rational decisions about their electoral choices. All these reasons were, of course, hotly disputed — as well as the question of the *quality* of working-class education. Throughout the nineteenth century middle-class reformers stressed that working-class education should not be too good. There was always a tension between those who genuinely desired real education for the masses and those who wanted a distinction kept between mass education and middle-class education. Thus, there were two kinds of education in existence in the nineteenth century, the major divisions between them being the social class barrier. Some radical reformers felt that the only democratic solution was to make middle-class education available to all, but most thought only in terms of a few working-class 'stars' being enabled to use middle-class education in order to become middle class. This is where part of the confusion begins. It is not clear whether the 'middle-class curriculum' was the transmission of middle-class culture or to what extent it was of potential value to all in our society. Some twentieth-century radicals now want to reject the traditional curriculum as bourgeois or middle class and say that for the working-class pupils we should devise a working-class curriculum. Others, while stressing that secondary schools curriculum is in need of a good deal of reform, would want to say that genuine education should cater for all classes of the population, and that to divert energies to constructing working-class curricula for working-class children is not only wasteful but is dangerously divisive and merely perpetuates the nineteenth-century barrier in a different way.

That is the historical background to the present argument — or at least part of it — about the content of the curriculum. It is quite clear that there are two traditions of education, and therefore of curriculum, operating especially at secondary school level, and one of the main reforms since the 1944 Education Act has been to try to bring these two traditions closer together. In many cases this has simply resulted in comprehensive schools taking some aspects of the old middle-class, public school and grammar school tradition and mixing it up with aspects of the old working-class elementary tradition. The result is almost inevitably a hotch-potch. Dissatisfaction with this hotch-potch has often led to teachers and other educationists wishing to reject the subject basis of the traditional curriculum and to look in other directions — one of them being the interest-based curriculum or non-curriculum which was discussed in Chapter 4. There is, however, a more philosophical problem which overlaps sociological issues about the content of the curriculum. This relates to the question raised earlier in this chapter and raised much earlier in the nineteenth century by Herbert Spencer,

namely, what knowledge is of most worth? Sociologists such
as M. F. D. Young have quite rightly criticized much educational research in the field of educational sociology and
psychology for *taking* problems rather than *making* them.
This means that researchers have been too ready to accept
what is taught in schools, and have gone on to ask 'Why do
some children fail – especially working class children?' This
has tended to result in what is often referred to as the deficit
theory of working-class children. That is to say if you
measure children's success and failure by any means at
school, using the conventional curriculum as a valid basis,
then working-class children are shown to be under-achieving.
M. F. D. Young and others have questioned this approach
and want to 'make' a new problem, namely to question the
validity of the traditional curriculum.

So far so good. But the issues become impossibly clouded
at this stage when those who want to question the worthwhileness of the traditional curriculum go much further and
begin to question the value of *any* kind of knowledge as
compared with any other kind of knowledge. This takes two
forms. There are those who want to say that working-class
knowledge and working-class culture are just as good as
middle-class versions of knowledge and culture; but there are
also those who go much further than this, and who want to
suggest that there are no good reasons for valuing any kind of
knowledge more highly than any other kind: they would
want to question the value of scientific knowledge, for
example, and would put forward arguments to suggest that
physics is just as suspect as, say, astrology. Once again one of
the problems here is to disentangle reasonable arguments
from very exaggerated arguments. One of the questions
which arises out of any relativist position is where does the
relativizing have to stop? To some extent most people are
relativists in our society today but the argument about the

curriculum in some cases goes to the lunatic extreme of relativism.

MARX

It is particularly ironic that some twentieth-century relativists claim to derive their inspiration from Marxism. This is ironic because although there are hints of a limited kind of relativism in Marx's writing he was essentially anti-relativist, and it is difficult to see how he could have been a revolutionary otherwise.

> Marx was, in fact, one of the originators of the sociology of knowledge, though in his eyes it was primarily a critical theory, intended to prepare the way for the constitution of a rigorous social science. Those who have followed Marx in this field have generally claimed too much for the sociology of knowledge, but they have nevertheless made important contributions to the history of thought, and especially of political thought (Bottomore and Rubel, 1963: 41).

Bottomore and Rubel were referring in particular to Mannheim but the same point could be made about many of the recent wave of sociologists of knowledge who have contributed much of the confusion about curriculum re-thinking.

The whole point of much of Marx's writing was that there does exist some kind of absolute truth, namely a 'scientific' view of man and the universe, as opposed to religious, philosophical or ideological views. Of course it is true that Marx argued (and most non-Marxist philosophers and sociologists would now agree) that a good deal of what passed for knowledge in any society is a social product of that society.

Marx also argued that much so-called knowledge is distorted by the ruling class at any particular time:

> The ideas of the ruling class are, in every age, the ruling ideas: i.e. the class which is the dominant material force in society is at the same time its dominant intellectual force. The class which has the means of material production at its disposal, has control at the same time over the means of mental production, so that in consequence the ideas of those who lack the means of mental production are, in general, subject to it. The dominant ideas are nothing more than the ideal expression of dominant material relationships, the dominant material relationships grasped as ideas, and thus of the relationships which make one class the ruling one; they are consequently the ideas of its dominance. The individuals composing the ruling class possess, among other things, consciousness, and therefore think. In so far, therefore, as they rule as a class and determine the whole extent of an epoch, it is self-evident that they do this in their whole range and thus, among other things, rule also as thinkers, as producers of ideas, and regulate the production and distribution of the ideas of their age. Consequently their ideas are the ruling ideas of the age. For instance, in an age and in a country where royal power, aristocracy, and the bourgeoisie are contending for domination and where, therefore, domination is shared, the doctrine of the separation of powers appears as the dominant idea and is enunciated as an 'eternal law'. The division of labour, which we saw earlier as one of the principal forces of history up to the present time, manifests itself also in the ruling class, as the division of mental and material labour, so that within this class one part appears as the thinkers of the class (its active conceptualising ideologists, who make it their chief source of livelihood to develop and perfect the illusion of the class about itself), while the others have a more passive and receptive attitude to these ideas and illusions because they are in reality the active members of this class and have less time to make up ideas and illusion about themselves. This cleavage within the ruling class may even develop into a certain opposition and hostility between the two parts, but in the event of a practical collision in which the class itself

is endangered, it disappears of its own accord and with it also the illusion that the ruling ideas were not the ideas of the ruling class and had a power distinct from the power of this class. The existence of revolutionary ideas in a particular age presupposes the existence of a revolutionary class. (*German Ideology 1845-6,* Vol. I/V, pp 35-36 quoted by Bottomore and Rubel, 1963, 93-94).

This is probably Marx's clearest statement about the influence of the ruling class on knowledge within a society. To some extent this view has now been accepted by historians and philosophers. It is recognized that every age interprets history, for example, through the perspective of the values and events of that particular time. The extent to which the ideas of any particular times are merely reflections of the ruling class is much more controversial but would not be rejected outright by many writers. But this is very different indeed from the extreme relativist position which says that each particular group tells its own story and that story is just as good as any other story. The great problem for all relativists is to draw a line where relativizing stops. If there is no such thing as an 'absolute' truth there is little point in trying to get closer to it by means of writing books, arguing or in other dialectical methods. In so far as Marx was a relativist he drew the line firmly at the boundary of science, and since one of his aims was to produce a scientific kind of history he would have included his history as 'the truth'. He thought that most of the nineteenth century history was a product of bourgeois society and therefore distorted, but *his* kind of scientific history was free from distortion: he thought it was true! It looks as though Marx's views on the relation between the relative and the absolute was much more complicated than the over-simplified versions adopted by some twentieth-century writers:

Aristotle's genius is shown precisely by the fact that he discovered, in the expression of the value of commodities, a relation of equality. Only the historical limitations of the society in which he lived prevented him from discovering the real nature of this equality. (*Capital 1* (1867) VA 1, p. 65, quoted by Bottomore and Rubel, 1963: 100).

Karl Mannheim, also in the Marxian tradition, held views on the sociology of knowledge which have been very influential but he himself was never led into the impossible position of negative relativism suggesting that any kind of curriculum would be as good as any other. Mannheim was in fact very interested in curriculum reform. He saw education as being one of the hopes for building a better society and in his *Freedom, Power and Democratic Planning* (1950) Mannheim put forward curriculum reform as part of his programme for freedom and democracy. This was in no way in conflict with his views on the sociology of knowledge which included what he referred to as relationism. Mannheim thought that society determined not only the appearance but also the content of knowledge (except for mathematics and some kinds of science). Mannheim was mainly concerned with the notion of 'ideology' which he used to denote the false or limited view of reality held by the ruling class. Mannheim felt that the ruling class view of reality was distorted since it was incomplete; it was also a conservative or reactionary view in as much as the ruling class had a vested interest in preserving the world as it was. Mannheim felt that different groups had different views of reality, each of them incomplete. He did, however, see a solution in training a kind of 'socially unattached intelligentsia' to transcend their limited view of reality, and, by acquiring a knowledge of the other views of reality, become detached in an intellectual sense.

Modern sociologists of knowledge such as M. F. D. Young,

however, go much further and state that not only is *all* knowledge socially constructed, but that this also implies that one version of reality is just as good as any other version, and even that rationality itself is merely a social convention. When relativists reach this stage they have in effect argued against producing any kind of curriculum. It is difficult to see how any teacher accepting that point of view could justify teaching anything in schools. Unless a teacher believes that there are some kinds of experience, some kinds of knowledge which are more important than the kinds of activities which children would indulge in if left to themselves it is difficult to see why teachers are necessary at all.

Less extreme views have been put forward sometimes as an attack on the conventional secondary school curriculum, sometimes as a more positive attack on the 'middle-class' curriculum. It is most necessary to distinguish between these two kinds of criticism of the traditional secondary school curriculum. I would certainly agree that most secondary schools' curriculum planning leaves much to be desired and lacks a suitable basic theory. I will develop this point in a more constructive way in a later chapter. But to say that the existing secondary school curriculum is inadequate does not mean to say that it is inadequate merely because it is middle-class, if indeed it is middle-class, which is arguable. There are strange mixtures of Marxist slogans and incomplete social analysis in the views of some of those who would replace the conventional curriculum by a working-class curriculum for working-class children. Such a view has been put forward in a variety of ways and emphasizing different aspects of the problem.

Jackson and Marsden (1962), for example, wrote about the middle-class nature of the grammar school world, and the difficulties which working-class children had in coping with various aspects of the school including the curriculum. This was a helpful book in analysing certain of the problems of social class and teacher-pupil relations. It did not, however, go into very great detail about the grammar school curriculum and did not offer very much constructive criticism of the curriculum and its possible alternatives for those children who found difficulties in adjusting to the grammar school. At this stage of the argument it might have appeared to be the solution merely to develop comprehensive schools with a different kind of curriculum as yet unstated. Since then Brian Jackson has from time to time suggested the advantages of a working-class curriculum for working-class children. In *Working Class Community* (1968) for example, Jackson outlined many of the positive aspects of working-class culture and made a plea for their retention; he was obviously concerned about the possibility of their being swallowed up by middle-class ways of life. I fully accept the arguments that there are positive aspects of working-class culture, such as sense of community, a high degree of co-operation rather than competition, a greater degree of warmth and personal relations, as well as interesting traditional activities such as pigeon-breeding, but it is difficult to see that these could form the basis of a total curriculum. Certainly they ought not to be ignored in curriculum planning but it does not seem to me possible to base the whole of a worthwhile curriculum on such activities any more than it would be possible to base a worthwhile curriculum on middle-class values and leisure-time interests. The whole point of education is to be much more universalistic in its intentions. This point will be developed in Chapter 8.

Other writers who appear to be advocating a working-class curriculum for working-class children are usually much less explicit in advocating particular curriculum content. Their criticisms of middle-class curriculum are in this respect negative criticisms. Also they tend to argue by implication rather than by direct assertion. Donald Swift (1965) outlined the problem of working-class educational under-achievement in terms of a culture clash in which pupils were at odds with the middle-class assumptions put forward by schools and teachers about tastes, career aspirations and leisure-time activities. Usually, however, this culture clash point of view is put forward without any constructive attempts to solve the problem. A similar approach occurs in Mays (1962) where there is the impression that the cultural gap between the pupils and the values of the school is so great as to make any solution extremely difficult. In his preface to Mays's (1962) work Lord Simey referred to the schools in the working-class areas as 'alien institutions'. Douglas Holly in *Society, Schools and Humanity* (1971) developed this idea of alienation of working-class pupils as the basis of his proposal which unfortunately becomes an argument for a different kind of curriculum for working-class pupils:

> But young people from established working class communities cannot be fully and personally involved in learning unless the school itself gives a deliberate centrality to the affective activities of art, design, creative writing, drama, craft work, gymnastics and sport. Whereas pupils from other areas can begin human realisation in cognitive activities these need to start from the feeling level and work outwards. The familiarity of the world of affect as the basis of all the relationships which matter to them give creative work an immediate priority over either social or physical science. In dealing with these adolescents teachers need a considerable inter-disciplinary competency in moving from one sort of activity into another — which suggests a staffing bias towards able non-graduates, art college trained teachers and a certain type of social science graduate. This sort of staffing and curricular policy indicates a need for schools custom designed for specific areas. Not only the general economic character of the neighbourhood but its specific regional, national and religious culture should be consulted in making the school open to a two-way educative current (Holly, 1971: 126).

Whilst not disagreeing with the last sentence of that quotation, I think the rest of it gets dangerously near to the Bantock position criticized in Chapter 2. The whole passage begs a number of questions about the needs of working-class children and their supposed 'affective' difference from middle-class children. This is not only highly questionable at an empirical level, it is also very dangerous. A final criticism of this passage is that it begs the relativist question about the worthwhileness of the activities quoted as compared with the disciplines or subjects of the 'normal' curriculum. There is an assumption here that the kind of activities which either working-class children are interested in (or which Holly thinks they might be more interested in) are just as valuable as academic knowledge. This is highly questionable and extremely dangerous.

The views of M. F. D. Young have already been referred to. Closely associated with his work is that of Nell Keddie who wrote one chapter of *Knowledge and Control* as well as editing a separate book *Tinker Tailor . . . The Myth of Cultural Deprivation* (1973). Young and Keddie are both influenced by the phenomenological school of sociology and object to the idea of knowledge as something 'outside' and therefore being imposed on children by teachers. As a supporting argument Keddie suggests that the current curriculum is often unacceptable to many children because it is derived from an alien sub-culture.

Culturally deprived children, then, come from homes where mainstream values do not prevail and are therefore less 'educable' than other children. The argument is that the school's function is to transmit the mainstream values of the society and the failure of children to acquire these values lies in their lack of educability. Thus their failure in schools is located in the home, in the pre-school environment, and not within the nature and social organisation of the school which 'processes' the children into achievement rates. This individualisation of failure — the perception of the problem as one in which teachers are faced with the difficulties presented by individual children — rests on a concept of mainstream culture that is by definition, in the use of indices such as income, occupation, education etc., a minority culture: the culture of the middle class which is then said to stand for 'society at large'. It is not a question whether the middle class culture (whatever that vague term means) is desirable or not, nor which of its values deserve to be transmitted to the next generation, but rather the recognition that mainstream and middle class values are one and the same thing and that neutrality in the construction of indices is impossible (Keddie, 1973: pp. 8-9).

We are back here to the question of whether the curriculum is middle-class, but, unfortunately, Keddie has not completed the examination of the question which she raises, namely the degree to which mainstream and middle-class values are one and the same thing. She is content to dismiss the question. I would not want to suggest that they are one and the same thing, but I think that Nell Keddie was mistaken in neglecting to explore the possibility of overlap, as well as the relation between working-class culture and mainstream culture. It is the area of overlap between all three (working-class, middle-class and mainstream) which could form the basis of a common curriculum. More of that later. Meanwhile, it may be worth examining the views of Harold Entwistle, himself a product of working-class culture and the English educational system, who has criticized Nell Keddie's views (Entwistle, 1976).

Entwistle points out the essential weakness in Keddie's (and others) argument. Keddie has rightly criticized the logic of the phrase 'cultural deprivation': since everyone has a culture how can anyone be deprived of their own culture? She goes on to argue that minority group cultures are adequate in their own right, and that any way of life has its own validity. This is the basis of her book *Tinker Tailor,* which Entwistle attacks on two counts — logical and historical. On the logical point he asks 'adequate for what?'. When Keddie states that any group culture is 'adequate in its own right' there is a logical necessity of stating adequate for something. It is at least a possibility that a form of cultural 'adequacy' may not extend very far either in terms of time or in place. A minority group culture which was adequate for certain purposes a hundred years ago may have ceased to be adequate for coping with twentieth-century society. It may also be possible that a rural minority culture ceases to be adequate in an urban situation. Unless Keddie completes her statement by saying adequate for what, her argment is meaningless. Entwistle's historical line of attack is the complaint that 'old-fashioned socialists as well as old-style sociologists of education have recently been perplexed by the thesis that cultural deprivation is a myth'. The whole tradition of improvement of working-class conditions rests on the assumption that there is something *wrong* with their conditions at the moment. If you add to that simple statement of fact the notion mentioned earlier in this chapter that economic inadequacy or sub-standard living conditions are likely to be related to other kinds of unsatisfactory conditions — mental, spiritual, aesthetic, etc. then the idea of deprivation takes on a new light. Entwistle makes extensive use of one of the founding fathers of Marxism to support this point of view. He quotes Engels *The Conditions of the Working Classes in England in 1844.* Engels had emphasized the demoralization of the workers who were deprived of humanity, having become 'the soulless factor of production', a mere machine. He described such workers as having been degraded to the level of animals. His description of life in 1844 included the brutalizing factory discipline, insanitary housing, loss of domestic skills, loss of the affections of family life, leisure spent in drunkenness and so on. Entwistle reminds us that the conventional 'enlightened' response to this kind of evidence was approval of legislation which protected children from certain aspects of their culture — especially work — and extended opportunities for education. In other words extending the possibility of escape from a life which was not 'adequate'. Entwistle suggests that the current relevance of Engels' account of working-class life is that it makes nonsense of the suggestion that no minority group culture can be regarded as deprived: 'only the conclusion that the working classes were culturally deprived can make sense of Marxism, and justify the disturbance of existing ways of life which is implicit in even modest social democratic proposals for reform' (Entwistle, 1976: 101).

Entwistle also makes a much more fundamental criticism of the relativist position:

> . . . for an educationist the essential limitation of the anthropological concept of culture lies precisely in its failure to discriminate normatively amongst items in this cultural aggregate. Culture conceived as the total way of life, unexamined, unrefined, unselective, cannot be an adequate conceptual tool for anyone concerned with intellectual, aesthetic or moral development . . . In its anthropological, descriptive sense, a culture must include strands which are technologically and economically disfunctional, others which aggravate social injustice, and yet others which offend aesthetic and moral values: anthropologically, the criminal sub-culture is a part of culture as are the drug culture and alcoholism. The political culture, for example, is a totality which must include Watergate and 'the unacceptable face of capitalism' as well as the Declaration of Independence, the Bill of Rights, Civil Rights Legislation and the Welfare State. As E. P. Thompson suggests in criticism of what he calls Eliot's 'sloppy and amateurish' versions of the anthropological concept . . . any characteristic list from the totality of cultural activities and artefacts must include items which reveal areas of

power and conflict: 'Strikes, Gallipoli, the bombing of Hiroshima, corrupt trade union elections . . . the massive distortion of news and Aldermaston marches' for example (p. 102).

It is therefore difficult to see any justification for social reform or revolution without organizing conditions of cultural deprivation.

> Even the voluntary pursuit of one's own education seems to require a perception of personal deficiency or inadequacy with reference to some aspect of the culture. Given that a person believed his skill or knowledge to be adequate it is difficult to see why he would take steps to further his own education. And this is true for anyone, irrespective of social class (p. 103).

There are two major points here. The first is that in some sense everyone is culturally deprived (but some are more deprived than others). Just as some individuals are more culturally deprived than others, so it may well be that some social *groups* are more deprived than others, given the mainstream development of our society along a certain cultural route. The second point is that some of the groups which we might judge to be more deprived than others may have been pushed into particularly difficult cultural situations. In my *Class, Culture and the Curriculum* (Lawton, 1975) I raised the possibility that there might be cultural dead-ends (for example it is difficult to see how gipsy culture can really survive in a full and meaningful sense in a society as urbanized as ours). I would now want to add to that the possibility of cultural 'disaster areas': it may be that the impact of slavery on cultural groups produces conditions of severe cultural deprivation. It may be that the worst aspects of urban slums — what Lewis has referred to as the culture of poverty — may also have enduring results. It would be over-pessimistic to think that such aspects of cultural deprivation cannot be rectified — by education or otherwise — but to pretend that they do not exist is doing a dis-service to the members of those minority groups. One of the least pleasant aspects of the current debate is that there is a strange kind of superior detachment about some left-wing sociologists' attitudes to those of a very different cultural group from their own. I find it difficult to listen quietly to highly literate people suggesting that working-class children may not 'need' to learn to read.

There is also a tendency to sentimentalize about sub-cultures rather than to indulge in an analysis of the values and attitudes as well as knowledge and skills of particular sub-cultural groups. Unexamined proposals about sub-cultural adequacy are likely to lead to more inequality rather than less. It should be stressed, however, that this view of education and culture is quite different from what has been condemned as the 'social pathology model'. The social pathology model assumes that something 'wrong' is transmitted by the family. This explains working-class under-achievement in schools by the fact that the family is incompetent and unable to pass on the right kinds of knowledge and skills. What I am suggesting is that *no* family is likely to be competent in passing on all the necessary values and skills. It may be that some families can conceal their incompetence better than others, but it would be quite wrong to see this mainly in terms of social class. The essential need is to analyse mainstream culture, so-called, and to see to what extent it does overlap both working-class and middle-class sub-cultural values and knowledge. Where there is considerable overlap between the sub-culture and the mainstream culture the task of education will be somewhat easier. But where there is less overlap, it does not mean that the school should not try to enable pupils to gain access to mainstream culture. This is surely one of the purposes of schools. If we accept the idea that schools have no responsibility to extend pupils' horizons in this way but only exist to allow children to develop within their own cultural framework, whatever it is, then it is very difficult to see why we need schools. We are back to the position that I put forward in the beginning of this chapter: that a major reason for the development of schools was that if individuals are to learn to cope creatively with their society, then schools have a job to do in encouraging children to see beyond their own immediate cultural horizons.

What then are the aspects of mainstream culture that schools should be concerned with? And why? In *Class, Culture and the Curriculum* (1975) I argued at some length that the curriculum was not (or should not be) a mere selection from middle-class culture, and that a good curriculum would be in a meaningful sense 'classless'. In order to make that statement less controversial, there are a number of issues that need clarifying in this debate. First, we need to distinguish between the typical, unreformed curriculum (primary or secondary) and an improved or reformed 'common curriculum'. (I will come back to the idea of curriculum reform later in this chapter, and at greater length in Chapter 8). I am by no means suggesting that the typical curriculum at the moment is a satisfactory one, and I would not wish to deny that some of the unsatisfactory aspects of curricula are concerned with social class. Part of the problem of reforming the curriculum is to distinguish between curriculum content and questions of middle-class taste and etiquette which have often loomed large — especially in grammar schools. But there is an enormous difference between saying that many teachers over-emphasize middle-class etiquette and values and saying that the curriculum itself is middle class, which is I think much less acceptable as a statement. There is also a difference between saying that 'the history taught in schools is too middle class' and 'history as a subject is middle class'. I would agree that many history syllabuses neglect certain important aspects of working-class history, or that working-class issues are treated in a biased way, but that is quite different from saying that history itself as a subject is bourgeois or middle class.

These are just a few of the distinctions which it is important to tidy up in order to make a little more sense of the discussion about culture and curriculum. Meanwhile, the question remaining concerns the worthwhileness of the kind of knowledge that I would expect to find in a selection from the culture in the form of a school curriculum. One of the main objections that relativists have to the conventional curriculum is that they question its validity. The argument is roughly that since knowledge is socially constructed, and since one social construction of knowledge is just as good as any other, then to accept or reject knowledge is a matter of individual taste, and one particular construction of knowledge should not be given priority by the school in the form of an imposed curriculum. The issue is rendered more complex, of course, by the fact that there are two issues involved here, one is the idea of knowledge and its validity, the other being the right of one individual − the teacher − to impose his view of reality or his social construction of reality on his pupils. They are aspects of the same problem and both of them serve to make life extremely difficult for a teacher who believes or even half believes in either of those two propositions.

The doctrine of cultural relativism first arose in connection with differences in moral behaviour between one society and another, and it may be helpful to begin at this point to see to what extent the arguments transfer from moral relativism to educational relativism. (There is of course a major difficulty here because when we speak of moral relativism we are essentially making comparisons *between* one society and another; but on questions of educational relativism we are normally making suggestions about knowledge *within* one particular society: this does make for certain difficulties for relativists which I will refer to again later in this chapter.)

The pre-anthropological writings of missionaries and explorers were characterized by a tendency to see cultural differences as cultural inferiority. For example, in a tribe where pre-marital chastity was not expected, this tended to be condemned as immoral behaviour and a sign that the particular society was inferior. In anthropology the culture concept changed that attitude very dramatically. For example, a typical statement in P. J. Pelto's book *The Study of Anthropology* (1965: 73):

> The customs and beliefs of people are often made more understandable by studying them in terms of the social inter-relationships among types of individual and group statuses and roles in social action. Painful ritual circumcision, knocking out of front teeth . . . may seem at first impression senseless and barbaric practices. If they are regarded simply as customs unrelated to other elements of cultural organisation, we can derive little understanding of these ceremonies. But these and other sorts of rituals begin to make sense as human acts when we view them as symbolic dramatisations of important status transitions experienced by individuals . . ..

Thus, anthropology encourages us to try to understand cultural differences rather than simply to think that they are silly or inferior in some other way, and this especially applies to questions of morality. However, even at this level there are difficulties. The question remains whether, despite differences in customs, there may not be higher order principles such as respect for persons which apply across the board to

all cultures. If not it is difficult to see how we could condemn the Nazis in Germany for killing six millions Jews. We
would have to put this down simply to an aspect of German
culture in the 1930s which we should attempt to understand
rather than condemn. So there may be, at the level of ethics,
principles or absolutes which we would want to keep in
mind. When we apply relativism to knowledge the difficulties
become even greater. 'Every human cultural system is logical
and coherent in its own terms, given the basic assumptions
and knowledge available to the given community' (Pelto,
1965: 71).

Pelto goes on to make the point that the differences in
thinking between primitive man and modern man lie in
fundamental assumptions about the world not by the fact
that primitive man is in any way 'illogical'. It is not illogical
for primitive man to believe that the world is flat or that the
sun revolves around the earth: within his knowledge structure
it is quite logical for him to believe that. Modern man knows
that the earth revolves around the sun because he belongs to
a different kind of knowledge structure. This is very
important if we are simply trying to point out that primitive
man should not be regarded as inferior to modern man. So
much is probably quite uncontroversial today, but the
modern sociologists of knowledge who are concerned with
relativizing educational knowledge want to push this further
and say that the Aborigine who thinks that the world is flat is
just as correct as the Russian who believes that the earth is
round. This would seem to be stretching relativism too far
and it is at this point where many philosophers accuse sociologists of neglecting two thousand years of epistemology in
their naive statements about knowledge. Richard Pring
(1972) has pointed out that the fact that we happen to make
distinctions in our culture between cats and dogs may be due
to certain *social* and linguistic conditions, but the fact that

we *can* distinguish between them has something to do with the *physical* characteristics of cats and dogs. In other words there are limits to the social construction of reality, and some social constructions may in fact be more correct than others.

It is partly for this reason, and partly because we all live in the same society that when we come to discuss the school curriculum in England now, it would seem reasonable to construct a curriculum out of the traditions or disciplines which have been built up in our society and which constitute our cultural heritage. This does not mean that children should be encouraged to accept everything within these cultural frameworks or disciplines as 'the truth', but it does mean that unless we encourage children to learn what discoveries previous generations have made in certain distinct areas such as science, mathematics, history, etc. then we are throwing away the benefits of belonging to a species which possesses the gift of language and can therefore transmit experience from one generation to the next. It should also be stressed that in each of the conventional disciplines that each generation does inevitably, to some extent, re-make the discipline. This then should be sufficient to counteract those attacks made by relativists that it is wrong to impose 'fixed' bodies of knowledge on children. If this were the case it would merely be bad teaching. An essential aspect of science, for example, is that the scientist has at his disposal a certain amount of knowledge and also the means of questioning that knowledge. But without the knowledge to question he is in a weaker position. It does seem very naive for relativists to argue that all teaching should begin with the child, and that any attempt to pass on knowledge from one generation to another by means of direct teaching is not only authoritarian but also in some way anti-educational.

Since these arguments may appear to have reached a rather abstract and unreal level, I will conclude this chapter with a discussion of the problem in concrete form, namely the events in William Tyndale School. This might have appeared equally well as a case study in the previous chapter on naive progressivism. Part of the confused picture of the William Tyndale events was of progressivism gone sadly astray, but part of it was also concerned with an abdication of curricular responsibilities, sometimes pursuing arguments associated with relativism.

WILLIAM TYNDALE SCHOOL: A CASE STUDY

One of the most interesting educational events of 1976 was the William Tyndale School Enquiry. This Islington Primary school under a new head had adopted a number of 'progressive' methods, which gave rise to conflict within the staff, conflict between staff and managers and eventually an official enquiry at the request of the ILEA. It was an important event partly because it raised, in a dramatic way, a number of issues of progressivism and relativism. As a case study it is also much better documented than most school scandals (for example Risinghill which was extremely badly reported). Before the end of the year 1976 three publications had appeared: the official report of the enquiry written by Robin Auld, QC, at the request of the ILEA *(William Tyndale Junior and Infant Schools Public Enquiry);* an account written by Terry Ellis and three of his colleagues (misleadingly called *William Tyndale, The Teachers' Story*); and a neutral version filling in some of the background written by two educational journalists, John Gretton and Mark Jackson, who had covered the case for the *Times Educational Supplement*

(William Tyndale, Collapse of a School – or a System?).

I will not attempt to tell the whole story again but will merely give a brief account which may illustrate the problem of a number of teachers who, in my view, genuinely wanted to generate a better kind of education for their pupils, but failed partly because of inadequate practical arrangements, but more importantly because they were working from false theoretical premises – in particular an exaggerated child-centred approach which gave children more responsibility than they could cope with and, of particular relevance to this chapter, an ill-considered relativistic attitude to knowledge and the curriculum.

I am immediately aware that my interpretation of the facts will please neither side: neither Rhodes Boyson nor the reporters of the popular press who saw the whole event as a left-wing Trotskyist plot to bring on revolution; nor the teachers themselves (i.e. the 'progressives') who claim that a successful experiment was deliberately sabotaged by re-actionary teachers, managers and a non-supportive local education authority. The evidence does not support either of these two versions, however. No evidence has ever been produced to show that the teachers were a part of a Trotskyist cell or were deliberately indoctrinating their pupils. On the other hand it is just as misleading to see their opponents as 'political' any more than anyone who interferes in education is automatically political. There were of course plenty of people who tried to make political capital out of the conflict – notably those who misleadingly used these events as an opportunity to condemn progressive education in general and even comprehensive schools in general, although William Tyndale School was a primary school.

I am not suggesting, of course, that the teachers at William Tyndale School were members of any organization or called themselves relativists. I am merely saying that one kind of

progressive view of education is closely related to what I have
described above as educational relativism. Teachers of this
kind have very often a commendable concern for the
freedom of individual children and they try to create a more
humane school atmosphere, rightly rejecting many aspects of
formal schools as oppressive. But this objection to harsh,
unpleasant institutions often spills over into an attack on the
curriculum — not just a bad curriculum but any curriculum.
This attack, or more probably neglect, takes place at the two
levels I have already outlined: that the curriculum is middle
class and therefore unsuitable for working-class pupils; that
knowledge is arbitrary and less important than the child's
own expression. This often develops into a view which says
that the *only* important function of education is to allow the
child to develop naturally. This is, as we shall see, at least
part of the William Tyndale story.

William Tyndale School is in an area of Islington which
used to be almost solidly working-class, but in recent years
has become popular with young middle-class and professional
people working in central London. Part of the trouble came
from middle-class parents who were not satisfied with the
school, and refused to accept answers they were given in
terms of progressive methods and so on. The head, however,
usually rejected the complaints of middle-class parents as
'trendies out for their own children' and the complaints of
working-class parents as 'working-class fascists' (Auld, p.
162). This might have been less damning if Mr Ellis could
have presented his own description of a primary school
curriculum which was superior to those which he had
implicitly rejected. But when he and his colleagues did produce a 'short and general statement of aims' it satisfied no
one, mainly because it was so short and so general that it
answered none of the questions that had been asked about it,
most of all by the parents.

They appeared unwilling to accept that their own conduct of the school might have been lacking, and made little attempt to explain their policies and methods to the parents who were clearly anxious about their children's education. The uninformative and resentful attitude that they adopted lost them irretrieveably the good-will of many parents and some of the managers (Auld, p. 137).

Gretton and Jackson, commenting on the unwillingness of the teachers to discuss methods and curriculum with managers and parents, accuse Ellis and his colleagues of being elitist and arrogant.

Like some medieval priest, the teacher is still wanting the parents to commit their children unreservedly to him, just as they were committed to their teachers by their parents — on the same grounds, that is, 'teacher knows best'. No allowance is made for any diversity of views among the parents, nor even for any expression of any views which might be allowed to influence the teachers (Gretton and Jackson, p. 49).

Later on in 1974 a longer document about the curriculum was produced at the request of the managers which was worth examining in a little more detail. The description of aims and curriculum is prefaced by a quotation from the well-known 1931 Report of the Consultative Committee, 'The curriculum is to be thought of in terms of activity and experience rather than knowledge to be acquired and facts to be stored.' This is often quoted and misinterpreted by those who advocate basing the curriculum on children's interests rather than on what children *need* in terms of knowledge and experiences. But the 1931 Report did not support the idea of extreme versions of the child-centred approach, 'We are . . . definitely of the opinion that it would be unnecessary and pedantic to attempt to throw the whole of the teaching of the primary school into the project form' (1931 Report, p.

104). And I am sure that Mr Ellis and his colleagues would not agree with many of the other statements about curriculum which also appeared in 1931, for example, 'It is . . . essential that provision should be made for an adequate amount of drill in reading, writing and arithmetic' (p. 140). Similarly the Plowden Report which the Tyndale teachers also give as the basis of their methods is nowhere as near the child-centred and relativist position as Ellis and his colleagues. To be fair to the teachers the aims do include the desirability of language expression and basic mathematics, but according to inspectors and other observers much was left to be desired in the children's competence in these fields. The integrated day was quoted as the basis of curriculum organization but this seems to have been an excuse for allowing children to do very much what they wanted to do. 'There was no adequate planning of the practical working of the scheme (that is the option scheme)' (Auld, p. 150). 'Very often a large proportion of the children did not, or were not encouraged, to take part in activities with much of a learning content in them. For example, many children were able to spend a good deal of their open session periods playing table tennis, draughts, or games out in the playground' (Auld, p. 151).

If teachers embark upon an unorthodox method of organization it is prudent, as well as professional, to keep adequate records of individual children's progress. This was not done. Unfortunately it is not enough for a teacher to have humane views about how to treat children, a good deal of hard work in organizing children's learning is also needed. This also apparently was rejected by the teachers concerned as unwarranted interference in children's development. Much was said about the interests of children and the needs of children but one of the school manager's children was eventually withdrawn from the school at his own request because he complained that he could find nowhere to read quietly. 'He was bored, there was little to read up to his level of ability, and apparently little encouragement to read; he could not concentrate on work that he wanted to do because of the constant noise and lack of order around him . . .' (Auld, p. 179).

Part of Ellis's and Haddow's policy for the school was that William Tyndale School should provide for pupils from poor backgrounds. There was in this policy a covert rejection of the traditional primary school curriculum as middle class and therefore unsuitable, but at no time was a reasonable alternative offered. Despite lip-service paid to language and mathematics in the aims, little effort was apparently made in these two directions. There is even a strange survival of social elitism in Ellis's thinking:

> During Mrs. Burnett's visit the steel band gave a concert to the school, which she attended. Seeing the school assembled, Mrs. Burnett noticed that it no longer appeared to contain 'the full range of socio-economic groups' and she remarked on this to Mr. Ellis. According to Mrs. Burnett he replied, that he was doing his best for the black and deprived children, but thought that it was not possible to cater for ordinary children as well. This remark disturbed Mrs. Burnett, and she made the point which she had made to him before, namely that, although she sympathised with his concern for deprived children, she felt that the state education system should be able to cater for all children (Auld, p. 193).

This is an example which I have commented on before of the tendency for teachers wishing to be kind to certain groups of children but in reality depriving them of a worthwhile set of educational experiences.

> Mr. Ellis and Mr. Haddow were convinced that children, especially those from poor backgrounds, should be given a wide measure of

choice, not only as to what they should learn, but also as to whether
and when they should learn. Mr. Ellis and Mr. Haddow believed that
children who were given that freedom would eventually find their
own way to learning with the aid and encouragement of the teacher
(Auld, p. 275).

It is difficult to see how children without a knowledge of
certain kinds of subjects and activities can find their way into
them unless they are very firmly guided by teachers. However, it looks as though the teachers themselves lacked any
kind of theoretical framework for evaluating knowledge and
experiences: whether they were aware of it or not they had a
relativistic view of knowledge — for them playing table tennis
was just as worthwhile an activity as reading.

Another aspect of the relativism implicit in the teachers'
attitudes was that they regarded subject barriers as arbitrary.
One way that this showed itself was that the library was
broken up and books were left around without being classified in any way. Many of the visitors and inspectors commented adversely on this. But one of the advantages of any
classification of knowledge into subjects — even an arbitrary
classification — is that children can be trained to find the
books they need to consult or read for themselves. Any
system is better than no system. The Tyndale teachers had
rejected the existing, conventional system of classification (of
books and knowledge) without putting in its place any alternative.

The clearest indication of relativism, however, comes from
the four teachers themselves:

The validity of experience for its own sake was stressed, running
counter to the idea that visits and other activities must be incor-
porated into an academic framework. The fact that they are going to
be forced, or cajoled, into academicism after an interesting activity
often spoils children's immediate enjoyment, which would seem to

defeat the primary purpose of the event. To the Tyndale staff the important thing was children being at the zoo, watching a great national event on television, or climbing a high tower and relishing the experience both at the time and afterwards — and not just the written evidence of having done it, which is often more for the benefit of visitors and inspectors (Ellis et al., pp. 46-47).

There are of course a number of questions begged here. The extreme child-centred naive assumption that the only purpose of an experience is for the child's immediate enjoyment; and the relativist assumption that watching the Derby on television was as valuable an experience as acquiring historical or scientific knowledge. No attempt is made to justify that judgement. The assumption is simply that horse-racing is as valuable, but no reason is put forward to support this view, apart from the implicit assumption that the child's enjoyment is the *only* arbiter of whether something is worth while or not. This is a strange position for teachers to get themselves in, since it virtually destroys the role of the teacher and the need to have schools. If the only purpose of a teacher in a classroom is to switch on the television set, without structuring that experience into some more general knowledge framework, then it looks as though the teacher is completely redundant.

This lack of theory on the part of the 'progressive' Tyndale teachers is very unfortunate because it would appear that most of them were genuinely interested in the well-being of their pupils. The fault was not entirely theirs, however. The ILEA could also be criticized for not giving sufficient structure and theoretical guidance. Gretton and Jackson make this statement, towards the end of their book (p. 120):

Mr. Auld had been gaily talking about 'efficiency' and 'suitability' but he was forced to recognise that, in practice — and London was no different in this respect from most other authorities — 'the authority has no policy

1. As to the standards of attainment at which its primary schools should aim;

2. As to the aims and objectives of the primary education being provided in its schools . . .;

3. As to the methods of teaching to be adopted in its schools.

Although the ILEA could not be accused of belonging to the relativist school of thought they had — at least at the time of the Tyndale Report — given far too little attention to the problem of relating some kind of theory of knowledge to curriculum planning and giving some guidance to their schools whilst at the same time permitting teachers within the schools a reasonable amount of autonomy in the classroom. Getting the balance right between a general curriculum framework and the freedom of the teacher is a difficult problem in the UK and one to which I shall return in Chapter 8.

6

THE DESCHOOLERS

In previous chapters I have tried to show that in the case of both the naive progressivists and the educational relativists, a logical result of their arguments would be to abolish schools altogether. If children can be relied upon to educate themselves, why have teachers? If all kinds of knowledge are equally good (or equally useless), then why have expensive institutions like schools to promote the transmission of knowledge? These kinds of arguments are sometimes put forward in favour of a policy of de-schooling, but there is another view associated especially with Ivan Illich who argues not only that schools are unnecessary but that they are positively harmful.

Illich begins his best-known book *Deschooling Society* (1971) in this way (p. 1):

Many students, especially those who are poor, intuitively know what the schools do for them. They school them to confuse process and substance. Once these become blurred, a new logic is assumed: the more treatment there is, the better are the results; or, escalation leads to success. The pupil is thereby 'schooled' to confuse teaching with learning, grade advancement with education, a diploma with competence, and fluency with the ability to say something new. His imagination is 'schooled' to accept service in place of value. Medical

treatment is mistaken for health care, social work for the improvement of community life, police protection for safety, military poise
for national security, the rat-race for productive work. Health,
learning, dignity, independence, and creative endeavour are defined
as little more than the performance of the institutions which claim
to serve these ends, and their improvement is made to depend on
allocating more resources to the management of hospitals, schools,
and other agencies in question. In these essays, I will show that the
institutionalisation of values leads inevitably to physical pollution,
social polarisation, and psychological impotence: three dimensions
in the process of global degradation and modernised misery.

It is important to recognize that Illich is attacking not just
schools, but the whole of our over-institutionalized, bureaucratized society. He does this particularly in the context of
the US and its influence over Latin America, but his arguments are intended to have world-wide applicability. It is
difficult to unpack the rhetoric from the substance of Illich's
writing, but I will try to summarize the arguments that he
puts forward to support his thesis that schooling is positively
harmful in the world today.

   Illich's first argument is that schools are people-processing
institutions   in   a   society   which   is   generally   over-
institutionalized.

I believe that a desirable future depends on our deliberately choosing
a life of action over a life of consumption, on our engendering a
life-style which will enable us to be spontaneous, independent, yet
related to each other, rather than maintaining a life-style which only
allows us to make and unmake, produce and consume – a style of
life which is merely a way-station on the road to the depletion and
pollution of the environment (*Deschooling Society*, p. 52).

Illich makes a distinction between institutions which are
manipulative and those which are 'convivial'. He condemns

manipulative institutions such as prisons, hospitals and schools, but accepts the need for convivial institutions such as telephone link-ups, public markets, sewage systems, drinking water, parks and side-walks. What is not clear is why he feels that it is impossible to make schools more convivial. One of the difficulties in analysing his arguments is that Illich nowhere makes clear why he objects to schools as schools rather than to schools *as they now exist* in an over-institutionalized society.

The second argument is that schooling, far from decreasing inequality, actually serves to increase it. This inequality exists both between rich and poor countries, and also within rich developed countries such as the US. Illich gives a good deal of detailed information about the cost of education in the US and the amount it would cost to produce equality in education even within the US. He also argues that in an institutionalized society, education serves to increase inequality between those who *succeed* in education and those who do not, and also between those who have certain kinds of educational advantage and privilege and those who do not. But, it is not clear whether Illich is blaming schooling for inequality or merely complaining, as I did at the beginning of this book, that schooling *so far* has failed to reduce inequality as much as many of us would like. The argument about the impossibility of under-developed countries having educational systems on such a lavish scale as has become customary in the developed countries is one which needs careful examination. However, there may well be arguments for making distinctions between compulsory initial education, the cost of which might easily be reduced, and additional optional education which might be catered for in a variety of ways.

Illich's third argument is related to his second: that schooling is divisive in an already divided society.

The very existence of obligatory schools divides any society into two realms: some time spans and processes and treatments and professions are 'academic' or 'pedagogic' and others are not. The power of school thus to divide social reality has no boundaries: education becomes unworldly and the world becomes non-educational (*Deschooling Society,* p. 24).

If we can disentangle the rhetoric from the argument, it may be that Illich has a point here in as much as schools have tended to exaggerate the difference between certain kinds of processes. I would go further and say that one of the damaging things that schools have done is not only to divide professions into 'academic' and 'non-academic', but within schools to use academic and non-academic as *labels* for children — a process which is extremely damaging to them in their future life. This, however, is a criticism of some schools *as they are,* not of schools as they might be. Most of us are dissatisfied with a number of aspects of the institutions as they exist now, but the real question is whether the general life-style of most people would be improved or made worse by the abolition of schools.

There is also a historic argument linked up with arguments two and three. The suggestion seems to be made that societies such as the UK and the US would have been better off without 'mass schooling'. This is an impossible question to answer. In the UK we would have to ask whether there would have been more or less inequality without, for example, the 1833 Education Grant, the 1870 Education Act and the 1944 Education Act. Although these 'reforms' have not solved the problem of inequality it is difficult to see how they could have made it worse, and it is at least arguable that the influence of education in the UK has diminished inequality. Illich's rhetoric is however very appealing to many who have heard or read such statements as:

Equal educational opportunity is indeed both a desirable and a feasible goal, but to equate this with obligatory schooling is to confuse salvation with the church. School has become the world religion of a modernised proletariat, and makes futile promises of salvation to the poor of the technological age. The nation-state has adopted it, drafting all citizens into a graded curriculum leading to sequential diplomas not unlike the initiation rituals and hieratic promotions of former times. The modern state has assumed the duty of enforcing the judgment of its educators through well-meant truant officers and job requirements, much as did the Spanish kings who enforced the judgment of their theologians through the conquistadors and the Inquisition (*Deschooling Society*, pp. 10-11).

This analogy between compulsory schooling and compulsory religion is one which runs through most of Illich's writing. Clearly he feels that just as some kind of Protestant Reformation took place which destroyed the power and monopoly of the church, so it is now necessary for society to overthrow the monopolistic power of institutionalized education. His argument is compelling at the level of criticism but much less convincing when it comes to alternatives. We shall deal with his proposals for alternatives to schooling below.

Illich's fourth argument is that teachers have too much power. The teacher, according to Illich, bases his authority on three different roles. The custodian, the preacher/moralist, and the therapist. The teacher/custodian guides his pupils through the rituals of rules and initiates him into adult life. He teaches him some skills and basic routine learning. The teacher-moralist is a substitute for parents, God or the state. He indoctrinates the pupil about what is right and wrong, and ensures that all children feel themselves to be children of the same state. The teacher-therapist feels that he has authority to delve into the personal life of his pupils in order to help them grow as persons. This view of the teacher is, of course, not original. Taylor and Musgrove in the UK have also pointed out the danger of a system of education which allows teachers too much power in a variety of roles within the school. But all this could be seen as a criticism of schools as they are; Illich does not demonstrate that schools inevitably have teachers wielding too much power.

The fifth argument against schools is that they merely socialize the young into an imperfect corrupt and capitalist society. This is a point which had been made before, at least as long ago as Marx, and more recently by the new sociologists of knowledge. It is a real difficulty because teachers are paid and employed by the state and there is always a danger that they might become the 'hired lackeys of the bourgoisie'. However, a defence might be made that the system does not appear to work very well in this respect, and that if schools are successful in being institutions of *education* rather than *training,* then the process of education necessarily equips the young with the means of reacting against their own teachers and the imperfection of their own society. If Illich thinks that the US is an unjust capitalist society, then education is necessary to equip people to understand that society better and to improve it. As usual, Illich is criticizing *schooling* rather than education. Those who might join in his attacks on schools *as they are* might still preserve their hopes for education. The answer might be to make schools into places of education and less like the institutions Illich so vividly describes. Some schools already are!

The sixth argument is that schools alienate the young and prepare them for even greater alienation in their work situation.

Alienation, in the traditional scheme, was a direct consequence of work becoming wage-labour which deprived man of the opportunity to create and be recreated. Now young people are pre-alienated by schools that isolate them while they pretend to be both producers and consumers of their own knowledge, which is conceived of as a commodity put on the market in school. Schools make alienation preparatory to life, thus depriving education of reality and work of creativity. Schools prepare for the alienating institutionalisation of life by teaching the need to be taught. Once this lesson is learned people lose their incentive to grow in independence; they no longer find relatedness attractive, and close themselves off to the surprises which life offers when it is not predetermined by institutional definition. And school directly or indirectly employs a major portion of the population. School either keeps people for life or makes sure that they will fit into some institution (*Deschooling Society*, pp. 46-47).

But this is a criticism of society itself rather than the institutions of education within it. It is rather unfair to complain about schools making alienation preparatory to life thus depriving education of reality and work of creativity when it is the conditions of life and work in our society which are much more to blame than schools themselves. Illich might be reminded that industrialists in England often criticize schools for not reflecting in a realistic way the true world outside schools. Schools are accused of *failing* to socialize the young and prepare them for the world of work. Schools are also criticized for paying too much attention to aspects of school such as creativity and critical awareness, and failing to prepare the young for the real world of work. If these criticisms are in any way true, then Illich's strictures about schooling must be much less appropriate. Alienation is certainly a problem in modern industrial societies and it is a problem in many schools. But in the UK it looks as though alienation in many schools is much less of a problem than alienation in the work situation. Perhaps Illich is expecting too much of schools? Schools cannot compensate for society, and schools should not be blamed for all the imperfections of society as a whole.

The final argument put forward by Illich is that schools are guilty of 'irrational consistency'. By this Illich seems to mean that modern industrialized societies set up a very elaborate technical bureaucratic machinery for various purposes, including education, and channel a good deal of money and energy for the purpose of schooling, but that this consistent effort is directed to irrational ends.

> Irrational consistency mesmorises accomplices who are engaged in mutually expedient and disciplined exploitation. It is the logic generated by bureaucratic behaviour. And it becomes the logic of a society which demands that managers of its educational institutions be held publicly accountable for the behavioural modification they produce in their clients (*Deschooling Society*, p. 68).

Illich may be quite right to criticize some of the worst features of US education, in particular the kind of accountability which manifests itself as 'behavioural objectives' and testing of various kinds. But this is a criticism of one type of schooling not of education in general, and not of schools as they already are in some places and might be in more places.

This is also related to Illich's rejection of the basic question in education: 'What should someone learn?'. Illich substitutes his own question: 'What kinds of things and people might learners want to be in contact with in order to learn?' (p. 78). This substitution of one question by another may be the crucial point in Illich's argument, but unfortunately he does not justify the substitution. As usual there is a general feeling pervading his writing that freedom is all-important, but Illich, as far as I know, nowhere examines the arguments that have been put forward to support the need for schools in our society. Basic to that argument is the question: '*What* should someone learn?' which Illich rejects. But if he is rejecting it he needs to argue the case very carefully. This he does not do. It is at least arguable that a good deal of the trouble with the schools that Illich criticizes, and the kind of schooling he does not like is that those schools have failed to answer this basic question, not that the basic question itself is a wrong one.

If Illich's arguments for deschooling society are unconvincing, his alternative proposals border on the ridiculous. His proposed solutions for a deschooled society which still has a need for learning seem to be totally unrealistic. They are much weaker, for example, than his criticisms of medicine and his proposals for alternative medicine in industrialized societies. Some of his ideas of alternatives to schooling are contained in *Deschooling Society,* but in 1974 he wrote a separate pamphlet *After Deschooling What?* Unfortunately Illich's proposals in both publications leave much to be desired. One of his ideas is that there should be 'learning webs' set up which would enable people to teach each other:

> Let me give, as an example of what I mean, a description of how an intellectual match might work in New York City. Each man, at any given moment and at a minimum price, could identify himself to a computer with his address and telephone number, indicating the book, article, film or recording on which he seeks a partner for discussion. Within days he could receive by mail the list of others who recently had taken the same initiative. This list would enable him by telephone to arrange for a meeting with persons who initially would be known exclusively by the fact that they requested the dialogue about the same subject (*Deschooling Society,* p. 19).

This suggestion is not only extremely bizarre, it also ignores a large number of practical difficulties. For example, how are most people going to read books if they have never been taught to read at schools? What kind of social groups are more likely to use such facilities? They might possibly be a substitute for expensive adult education classes, but as a serious alternative to schools the proposal is a complete non-starter. Illich's other suggestions include 'reference services to educational objects', that is elaborating access to libraries, museums and so on. 'Skill exchanges', personal learning by face to face contact; 'peer matching', a communication network such as the one described for New York City above, and finally 'reference services to educators at large'. This last suggestion would be a kind of directory giving the addresses of professionals, para-professionals and free-lancers who would give, or charge for, their services to the public at large.

None of this, however, really adds up to a sensible alternative to the kind of institutionalized education which we have at the moment. Whilst I would be the first to admit that there are many deficiencies in the present system, it does not seem to me that Illich's alternatives are in any way acceptable. Illich has put forward many cogent, if over-colourful, criticisms of a large number of schools (especially in the US) but he is much less convincing when he argues for de-schooling or the dis-establishment of schools. This is an unrealistic view because he puts forward no reasonable system to cater for the needs of the young people to learn how to cope with a modern industrial society and to acquire the complex knowledge that is available within it. The major criticism against Illich is therefore that he fails to analyse the concept of education and the educational needs of most people in any modern society.

Illich's contribution has been to illustrate the deficiencies and evils of many schools, and the important dangers existing in large, bureaucratized institutions. In some respects he was merely echoing — in his own very colourful style — the attacks on American education by such writers as Everett Reimer and Jules Henry. But here it is necessary to make a distinction between Illich's views on deschooling (or as he more recently describes it 'dis-establishment of schools') and Jules Henry's views, which might be described as anti-schooling. A good deal of Henry's writing (and others such as Reimer and Postman) are arguing against a number of evils they see in US society and reflected in an uncritical way in American education. These criticisms would include the cult of efficiency, the uncritical use of tests and testing, the factory model of schooling which treats pupils as commodities to be processed rather than human beings to be developed, and the behavioural objectives model of curriculum and evaluation. But having admitted that much is wrong with many or even most schools in the US we still have to work out what the solution is. This involves asking whether most children would be better or worse off without schools. There are many people in education, including myself, who would say that they went to bad or indifferent schools but are still better off having been to those schools than they would have been without them. We are left with an important question, i.e. how to 'unfetter' children in schools but still give them the kind of education which they need in order to understand and enjoy modern society.

A more constructive approach to the radical reform of education is that of Paulo Freire. Freire is just as critical of schools as Illich but much less pessimistic about the possibility of change. The difference in approach has been discussed in an interesting way by David Hargreaves in a somewhat neglected paper 'Deschoolers and New Romantics' (1974). One of the difficulties in this area is that many educationists and teachers who are dissatisfied with schools as they are, and desperately want reform of some kind may be seduced by the compelling language used by Illich. It is therefore all the more important to distinguish between the arguments of the deschoolers and those who advocate radical reform in education without the dis-establishment of schools and other educational institutions. Hargreaves points out that whereas the deschoolers want to abolish schools and other institutions together with their close control over what is held to constitute education, the new romantics on the other hand propose reformist alternatives:

> Their dominant concern is to reformulate the content of the curriculum and the nature of pedagogy, but they do not seek to change the basic institutional structure of schooling. Their analysis is thus for the most part at the micro-sociological or social psychological level (Hargreaves, 1974: 186).

Hargreaves also points out that the confusion between these two groups is confounded still further by the fact that some writers like Paul Goodman seem to have anticipated both groups to some extent in his *Compulsory Miseducation* (1962). Others, like John Holt, have changed position. Holt's first book *How Children Fail* (1964) was a reformist book whereas his more recent *Freedom and Beyond* (1972) shows that he has been influenced by Illich and the deschoolers and has moved over into their camp. The new romantics on the other hand do have a common philosophy to some extent and it would be difficult, according to Hargreaves, to distinguish them from other contemporary innovators such as the advocates of open schooling and the community school.

Hargreaves's conclusion, after reviewing the arguments put forward by Illich, Reimer and others, is that they are a group of impractical visionaries. An American commentator, Phillip Jackson, in 'An American View of Deschooling' (1972), has condemned them in rather different terms by suggesting that Illich is both misinformed and irresponsible (misusing sociological or semi-sociological data in a cavalier unscholarly way). I would go even further and accuse the deschoolers of being Utopian, using the word in the pejorative sense employed by Popper in *The Open Society and Its Enemies* (1945). Illich condemns present-day society and its schools, but instead of proposing the kind of piecemeal social engineering which Popper advocated, Illich goes all out for a vision of a totally different society which would involve abolishing our schools and other kinds of institutions. This is just the kind of dangerous totalitarian thinking that Popper so convincingly criticized in the early post-war period.

Hargreaves contrasts the deschoolers with the New Romantics whom he identifies by two criteria: their reformist position and their focus on the micro rather than the macro level of change. A further distinction is that, unlike Illich, most New Romantics write on the basis of classroom experience. On the other hand Hargreaves criticizes them for a tendency to argue from personal anecdotes (or second-hand anecdotes), for too much emotional language, and a failure to develop sustained arguments or to marshall their evidence in a satisfactory way. Although the New Romantics are profoundly dissatisfied with some kinds of schools they do *not* over-generalize and attack *all* schools and *all* teachers. The romantic qualities which Hargreaves describes include the idea that learners are *naturally* motivated, that freedom and choice should be emphasized in education, and that traditional methods of teaching encourage the wrong kind of learning. Hargreaves reviews their ideas sympathetically, and clearly hopes that they will become more influential. Unfortunately, he is perhaps too tolerant of the New Romantic tendency to underestimate the importance of curriculum planning. In my terms some New Romantics get much too close to the naive progressivism and relativism which I criticized in Chapters 4 and 5.

Freire does not belong in either camp. Although his name is often linked with that of Illich he is not a deschooler, and although he criticizes some kinds of curriculum he does not appear to be totally opposed to planning. Freire's 'banking concept of education' is often quoted; by this he means that teachers tend to see knowledge as a commodity to be transported from one person to another. Although he condemns this attitude, he does not deny the importance of some kinds of knowledge especially political knowledge. Freire is an important educational thinker, but it is not clear to what extent his ideas can be transferred from teaching adults in Latin America to younger pupils living in technological societies of a much more developed kind. The foreword by Richard Shaull to *Pedagogy of the Oppressed* (1970) makes this point clearly:

> At first sight Paulo Freire's method of teaching illiterates in Latin America seems to belong to a different world from that in which we find ourselves. Certainly it would be absurd to claim that it should be copied here. But there are certain parallels in the two situations which should not be overlooked. Our advanced technological society is rapidly making objects of most of us and subtly programming us into conformity to the logic of its system. To the degree that this happens, we are also becoming submerged in a new 'culture of silence' (*Pedagogy of the Oppressed,* p. 13).

In my view what can be tranferred from Freire's Latin American experience to the Western developed world is at the level of pedagogy rather than of curriculum. Much of what Freire has to say about the banking concept of education makes very good sense as a criticism of traditional teacher-pupil relations, but it does not solve the problem of what children need to know in order to develop satisfactorily in our society.

> In the banking concept of education, knowledge is a gift bestowed by those who consider themselves knowledgeable upon those whom

they consider to know nothing. Projecting an absolute ignorance on to others, a characteristic of the ideology of oppression, negates education and knowledge as processes of enquiry. The teacher presents himself to his students as their necessary opposite; by considering their ignorance absolute, he justifies his own existence. The students, alienated like the slave in the Hegelian dialectic, accept their ignorance as justifying the teacher's existence — but, unlike the slave, they never discover that they educate the teacher.

The raison d'etre of libertarian education, on the other hand, lies in its drive towards reconciliation. Education must begin with the solution of the teacher-student contradiction, by reconciling the poles of the contradiction so that both are simultaneously teachers *and* students.

This solution is not (nor can it be) found in the banking concept. On the contrary, banking education maintains and even stimulates the contradiction through the following attitudes and practices, which mirror oppressive society as a whole:

1. The teacher teaches and the students are taught.
2. The teacher knows everything and the students know nothing.
3. The teacher thinks and the students are thought about.
4. The teacher talks and the students listen — meekly.
5. The teacher disciplines and the students are disciplined.
6. The teacher chooses and enforces his choice, and the students comply.
7. The teacher acts and the students have the illusion of acting through the action of the teacher.
8. The teacher chooses the programme content, and the students (who were not consulted) adapt to it.
9. The teacher confuses the authority of knowledge with his own professional authority which he sets in opposition to the freedom of the students.
10. The teacher is the subject of the learning process, while the pupils are mere objects.

(*Pedagogy of the Oppressed,* pp. 46-47.)

This is an important guide to teacher-pupil relationships or, if you prefer, pedagogy. I have suggested, however, that it evades the major issue in mainstream education *in schools* because it does not deal with the question of *what* should be taught. With all respect to Freire and his experience of adult education, there is a considerable difference between adult education and the needs of much younger students. There is also some confusion in Freire's own argument. First, his description of the banking concept and the ten points listed above give us a parody of teaching in schools rather than what usually happens. Secondly, Freire nowhere deals adequately with his own point 9: 'the teacher confuses the authority of knowledge with his own professional authority'. This is a key issue in planning a curriculum for schools. It has appeared to some commentators that Freire is opposed to the idea of curriculum. One of the unfortunate aspects of his writing is that this is never made clear. What is clear is that there is a 'hidden curriculum' implicit in a good deal of what Freire has to say although he sometimes seems to oppose the idea of a teacher guiding students' activities in any way. But Freire's hidden curriculum − in the sense of an unstated agenda − seems to include a number of important areas of knowledge. I have already mentioned politics; Freire obviously considers this to be an essential kind of knowledge to produce 'humanisation of the oppressed' and to give his adult students a greater degree of control over their own environment by means of a heightened awareness of their social situation. Other aspects of the unstated curriculum also emerge from time to time; for example, on page 64 Freire discusses men's 'incompleteness'. But to have a concept of incompleteness it would also seem to be necessary to have a concept of 'completeness', and the question which we have to ask is 'what kind of *knowledge* makes an incomplete person more complete'. Later in the same section, Freire writes about understanding 'reality' as the basis of all education and on page 94 he suggests the concept of culture as the basis of many educational dialogues. Freire also seems to approve of the idea that man cannot understand his present conditions without an understanding of history.

The adult education tutor can avoid the issue of a planned curriculum and can rely almost entirely on students' spontaneous problems, but it is much more difficult to operate on this basis in a school situation. In schools we need to make Freire's hidden curriculum into something much more explicit. I suggest that this is possible without falling into the trap of the 'banking concept of education'. However, it is easy to accept Freire's criticisms about much educational practice contained in his idea of 'banking', but it is by no means clear exactly what Freire means by this. I would want to distinguish between the banking concept of education at the pedagogical level and what the implications are at the level of curriculum planning. Both Illich and Freire have failed to deal with the problem of authority in education. Both tend to dislike some kinds of authority, and fall into the easy trap of condemning all authority in education; but Freire, for example, makes an implicit claim to be an authority. He is an authority on the education of illiterate peasants; he tells us how to teach them; he gives us a good deal of advice. If he did not think he was an authority why would he bother to write a book about it? Of course there is much wrong with teaching style or pedagogy at all levels of education, but this should not be allowed to rule out the idea of the authority of the teacher as curriculum planner; one of the most important duties that teachers have is to avoid wasting their pupils' time: they have to justify the time spent in education by offering a worthwhile curriculum. It is impossible to learn all that it is necessary to know as a result of spontaneous dialogues. We need some kind of curriculum planning. To some extent the teacher cannot avoid being *an* authority on what he teaches even if (to use Richard Peters' very useful distinction) he is unhappy about his position in authority.

This is one aspect of the problem of authority in education which neither Illich nor Freire attempted to solve. Clearly Illich, Freire and many others discussed in this chapter are very uneasy about authority in society generally, and in schools in particular. This is especially so in the case of Illich and his dislike of institutions. But there is a dangerous tendency to confuse authority in education with being authoritarian. I think it might be useful at this stage to try to clarify this issue before going on to the next part of the argument.

One of the features of democratic societies is that we are rightly suspicious about authority. During the last few hundred years there has been a shift of authority away from what Weber called 'traditional' authority to 'legal/rational' authority in our society as a whole. More recently this has been reflected to some extent in education. Weber suggested that the traditional kind of authority consisted of an acceptance of the authority of 'masters' or leaders. The 'legitimate' feeling of subordination was based on custom: the authority had been accepted without question for ages past; it was thought that it was 'right' to obey that kind of person − a king or a superior of some kind. This was an unthinking, non-controversial acceptance of authority, and it was − in those situations − considered wrong even to doubt the basis of authority. In English history the medieval king could exercise arbitrary authority, limited only by the framework of custom.

In contrast to this, legal/rational authority, according to Weber, depends on the existence of *good reasons* for accepting the authority. The authority is part of an institution which is beneficial in some way to those obeying the authority. It is in accord with more general rules such as fairness, justice, or the need for order.

The growth of rationality in our society has had all sorts of consequences which are directly or indirectly connected with education: for example, examinations for the civil service — people get jobs on the more 'rational' grounds of ability rather than the 'traditional' grounds of being a member of a certain kind of family. Peters (1966) has developed this typology of kinds of authority, and within the framework of rational authority has suggested that in education a person can be *in* authority by reason of his possessing a certain institutional position (for example a headmaster or a teacher) or he can be *an* authority by reason of his expertise in a particular subject area. The whole tendency of modern education is to play down the kind of '*in* authority' relationship and to stress, as Freire does, that teachers are also in a learning situation and that teachers very rarely know everything. Nevertheless, in school education (as opposed to adult education) it is difficult to avoid the 'in authority' idea altogether — children are compelled to go to school and teachers are placed by the state in authority over them and this, whether we like it or not, does involve some custodial duties as well as purely educational ones. However, the main point is that for a teacher to be a teacher in any meaningful sense, he has surely to be *an* authority. He may, out of tact or courtesy, wear his authority lightly, but unless he is an expert or at least more of an expert than his students, he is likely to waste their time. Illich and Freire appear to be confusing these two kinds of authority when they discuss various educational problems, and in particular when Freire uses his idea of the banking concept of education. In this respect Illich may be more logical than Freire. Illich wishes to abolish schools and therefore could abolish the problem of 'in authority', Freire apparently would not wish to do this. What neither Illich nor Freire has managed to do is to clarify the idea of being *an* authority.

I have dwelt on Freire for some time in order to illustrate the important point that it is possible to be a radical educationist without throwing overboard all the ideas of incorporating an improved pedagogy into schools. Certainly there is a good deal wrong with the way that pupils are taught in many schools, even if they are not as bad as Freire and Illich would suggest. However, the problem that remains is one of curriculum. Given that there is much wrong with educational programmes in schools at the moment, given that Freire is right in suggesting that education in the past has concentrated too much on socialization and not enough on 'humanization' or the development of human consciousness, the problems of curriculum remain. We need to devise a programme in schools which will enable students to develop in this way. We cannot escape from the problem by placing the whole burden of reform on the question of pedagogy or pupil-teacher relationships. In a compulsory system someone inevitably has the burden of working out what kinds of knowledge and what kinds of experience are necessary for pupils to acquire humanization or to develop consciousness. It is far too easy to avoid this problem altogether by condemning any attempt to plan education under the somewhat misleading label of 'banking education'.

A. H. Halsey has recently (1976) discussed two basic theories about education and society in an interesting paper, 'Is a Society Liberated or Repressed by its Educational System?', which was first presented as an Open University programme and later re-written for the *Times Higher Education Supplement*. Halsey suggests that there are two basic theories about education and society. The first is that education is

The rock on which a modern, prosperous and complex civilisation is based. It creates new knowledge, ensures that people can use advanced scientific cultures and separates individuals into the jobs they are able to do well. The second theory is that education is nothing but an organisation of control, stupifying the majority into acquiescence with the interests of the powerful, impoverishing the lives of ordinary men. If men are to be free, to be creative and to be rich in the things that matter, they must rid themselves of the professional pedagog and the oppression of organised educational bureaucracies which make them both revere false knowledge and spend ever longer proportions of their lives in attempting to acquire it.

In this chapter I have examined the views of Illich and others who clearly believe that education is harmful (Halsey's theory 2), and I have also tried to show that although some schools now might deserve Illich's criticisms, there is no reason why schools generally should not move towards Halsey's theory 1. In other words, I recognize that schools should operate with theory 1 but many still have some of the characteristics of Halsey's theory 2. Halsey concludes his paper in this way:

> From Illich, we have a vivid picture of such an ideal world, but with no convincing plan as to how we might reach it. From Freire we have an account of educational means towards much the same end, but embedded in a theory of revolutions which I find unacceptable. Formal systems of education must play a vital part in the road to greater freedom and less inequality, but this destination can and should be reached by political action other than revolution. It requires political will to be sure, but it is possible within the framework of traditional Western parliamentary democracies.

In the next chapter I describe the Labour Party's attempt to find a democratic framework and the reason for their partial failure. In Chapter 8 I will make some personal suggestions for relating theory to democratic policy-making.

7

THE LABOUR PARTY: FAILURE TO TRANSLATE SLOGAN INTO POLICY

I started writing this book with five 'villains' in mind — the false doctrines which gave Chapters 2 to 6 their titles. There are probably more, but there is another chapter which needs to be written which is not so much about a villain as a failed hero — the Labour Party. Many people would claim that the Labour Party could and should have achieved a much higher level of social justice in education had it lived up to its ideals, and if a higher priority had been given to education since 1945. This is partly true, but there are also more serious and deep-rooted problems at a theoretical level. For instance, we might want to ask why is it that the policy of laissez-faire, which has been condemned by the Labour Party in most spheres of social and economic life, has survived so long in education, particularly at the level of curriculum planning (where non-planning has been claimed as a virtue). The conventional answer given by politicians is usually couched in phrases about freedom of the teacher, autonomy of the schools, etc. But the real answer is a lack of policy in this area, and behind that lack of policy a lack of any theory of socialist or social democratic education. In the next chapter I

want to make a few suggestions or notes 'towards a democratic theory of curriculum planning', but before beginning
that, it would be useful to outline the reasons for the failure
of the Labour Party to produce such a theory and therefore
to produce coherent educational policies.

On far too many occasions the Labour Party has acted as
the executive agent carrying out the policies of other parties,
Liberal and Conservative, and has failed to produce policies
of its own, even regarding it as prudent to adopt a bi-partisan
approach to education. Why? One reason is a misplaced belief
that education, like religion, ought to be kept out of politics;
a second is the split within the Labour Party on important
educational issues; a third is the difficulty of generating a
theory of education, which is much more difficult than
health or social welfare. These three reasons have obvious
interconnections and overlap a good deal, but it may be
useful to bear them in mind separately before going on to a
more chronological account of why the Labour Party went
wrong in educational matters, especially social justice in
education.

On the question of keeping education out of politics, this
has always been one of the great heresies of Labour Party
politicians. It has been insufficiently stressed by those on the
left in politics, that everything in education is essentially a
political activity, whether schools tend to preserve the status
quo in society or to advocate change, such intentions are
inevitably political. Politicians on the right have got away
with accusing the Labour Party of using education to promote social change while they blatantly use education to
preserve the status quo and claim that this is non-political. C.
P. Trevelyan, the first Labour President of the Board of
Education, in 1924, set the pattern for his successors by
adopting a style of ministerial behaviour which was in no way
different from Liberals and Conservatives, including his Tory

predecessor, Lord Eustace Percy. This was the beginning of a bi-partisan educational policy which certainly continued throughout the first two Labour governments, and many would argue has continued ever since then with one or two minor exceptions. Thus, Labour spokesmen for Education have found themselves, up to and including 1944, carrying out policies which had been predetermined for them by the previous Conservative administration. What has tended to happen when Labour is in office is that minor changes in direction are made rather than fundamental educational reforms.

The second reason I suggested for failure in educational matters was that the Labour Party was itself internally split on fundamental questions of educational ideology. Before the Labour Party was established at the beginning of the twentieth century two very different views were already developed within the Labour Movement. In 1897 the TUC had demanded secondary education for all, condemning the segregation of elementary and secondary schools, and the elitist basis of the grammar school curriculum. But the Fabian Society, under the disastrous direction of Sidney Webb, had pursued a policy very much in the Liberal Utilitarian tradition, justifying selection on grounds of economic and social efficiency. This is a distinction I made in Chapter 3 between those who want real social justice in education and those who talk about social justice but in fact adopt a completely meritocratic outlook. This distinction within the Labour Party has been blurred and has confused a number of important policy decisions such as comprehensive schools and their organization.

The third reason I suggested was that it is much more difficult to generate a theory of education than it is to have ideas about other social and economic matters. There have in fact been no socialist theorists of education within the

Labour Party. Many people would claim R. H. Tawney as an educational theorist, but his theoretical contributions were almost nil and he too often fell into the trap I have already discussed of merely carrying out existing Liberal policies. (Examples will be given later in this chapter.) Similarly, Anthony Crosland whose book *The Future of Socialism* stimulated an immense amount of thinking within the Labour Party, had little to say about education at a theoretical level and, in my opinion, although the book as a whole was important, I think that the sections on education are by far the weakest and most conservative. The problem is that if Labour politicians lack a theory of education and society then when they are in office they have to play the game according to the existing rules. And the existing rules are laid down by the officials of the Ministry of Education or, more recently, the Department of Education and Science. Inevitably these basic guidelines are of a conservative nature. I would go further and suggest that even when policy documents written by officials appear to be forward-looking they are in fact often a generation or so out of date in terms of social and educational thinking. Once again I will make detailed reference to this later in the chapter.

It has been suggested that

> there can be no practical socialist educational policy except in conjunction with a general policy making for social equality in every part of the structure of communal life. That is why socialist educational ideas are so difficult to disentangle from general socialist conceptions . . .. (G. D. H. Cole, quoted by M. Parkinson, 1970: pp. 3-4).

But this sensible interrelationship of social and educational theory can become barren if there is no clear idea of what education means for a socialist, and what social purposes

education means for a socialist, and what social purposes
tional ideas exist in conjunction with general policy-making
should *not* be interpreted as meaning that there is no need
for a socialist educational theory.

It is difficult to know where to begin the story of Labour
and education since, although the Labour Party was not
officially started until 1906, the Labour Movement had a
much longer involvement in education as Brian Simon (1960)
has shown, and many would say that the Labour Party
actively began with the formation of the Labour Representation Committee in 1900. It may then be helpful to confine
our discussion mainly to the twentieth century and to those
events which took place just before the birth of the Labour
Party. The end of the nineteenth century had been marked
by a series of decisions, both administrative and judicial,
which had effectively limited elementary education to a low
level and had prevented it from becoming an alternative form
of secondary education of a technical and scientific kind (see
Chapter 3). A wedge was driven between elementary and
secondary education, keeping them apart, in a way which was
quite in harmony with nineteenth-century Liberal and Conservative policies but which should have been obnoxious to
twentieth-century democratic ideas. In 1897 the TUC had
demanded secondary education for all, but the Fabian
pamphlet *The Education Muddle and the Way Out* (1901)
took a very different line, justifying selection and segregation
for reasons of social and economic efficiency, and supporting
the policy of differentiating between elementary and
secondary curricula. This was the beginning of the most
serious ideological split within the Labour Party. So similar
were Sidney Webb's views to the official Conservative line on
this that in January 1901 Sir John Gorst, the Conservative
education spokesman in the House of Commons, obtained
proof copies of the Fabian manifesto *The Education Muddle*

and the Way Out and distributed them to support his own
policy for preserving the separation between elementary and
secondary schools and providing a 'ladder' by means of
scholarships. In the House of Commons the two Labour
Representation Committee members, Hardie and Bell,
opposed this policy and much of the Labour Movement at
this time was on their side, but an influential body of opinion
within the Labour Party had established a non-socialist tradition which was later to become the dominant form of thinking within the Party. The 1902 Act, which is often seen as a
great step forward in providing state secondary schools, was
in fact part of a reactionary policy of keeping elementary and
secondary schools firmly apart. The Labour Movement
generally saw this Act as a piece of class legislation, much in
keeping with the anti-union policies of the Tory Government
after the Taff Vale Judgement in 1901. In 1907 the measures
establishing state secondary schools were followed up by a
modest proposal to set up scholarship links between elementary and grammar schools. This was also greeted differently by the two wings within the Party. Most felt that a
few scholarships were a poor substitute for real education for
all working-class pupils, but many others felt that it should
be welcomed as a step in the right direction by providing
some able working-class pupils with a route to middle-class
education. The feeling that there should be genuine education for all pupils, however, continued during discussions on
the 1918 Act when Ramsay MacDonald and F. W. Goldstern
protested against a secondary school system which effectively
'skimmed off the cream' from elementary schools but did not
provide a satisfactory system for all children. However, other
Labour Party members such as Snowden supported the
system which had brought them up the hard way — Snowden
even objected to the end of the half-time system of education
in 1918.

Parkinson's view of the Labour Party and education in 1918 was that

> Although the Party was generally committed to the idea of educational reform, it had not developed any coherent, long-term policies. It tended to react in an ad hoc way to issues as they arose rather than attempting itself to force the pace of reform (p. 8).

In 1918 the Labour Party did however publish *Labour and the New Social Order* which called for reorganization of the whole education structure on the basis of social equality — but it did not include secondary education for all in its demands. At this early stage the confusion between variety and inequality was in evidence.

Another way of identifying the different ideologies existing within the Party was in the use of metaphor (always illuminating in educational debate): the Labour meritocrats (together with the Tories) tended to talk of a 'ladder of opportunity' from elementary schools to secondary schools, enabling clever working-class children to rise educationally and socially; on the other hand, the egalitarians within the Party were beginning to talk of the 'broad highway' — a route to a better life for *all* pupils. But even this was originally a Liberal idea: in 1913 a Liberal MP, Mr Whitehouse, criticized those who regarded secondary education as appropriate to a certain rank or class:

> We ask that there should be no further tendency to crystallize separate systems of education for separate systems of society, we ask that elementary education should not be regarded as a system complete in itself, or as a system on which to fit a coping-stone of the higher elementary school or so-called evening classes ... we ask that elementary education be regarded as the first stage of the educational highway, and every child leaving the elementary school should pass along that educational highway to some secondary

institution. (*Hansard,* 10 April 1913, quoted by Banks, 1955: pp. 117-18).

The idea of one broad highway became part of the Labour Party egalitarian thinking which was a totally different concept of secondary education from that of the Labour meritocrats and Tories. In 1922 the idea of the broad highway approach was encapsulated in *Secondary Education for All,* a Labour Party document edited by R. H. Tawney. This is a remarkable publication in many ways, and is often hailed as a turning point in English educational history. But it was not without weaknesses as a policy document. It certainly provided very powerful criticisms of the abuses and shortcomings of the existing system: it condemned the idea of secondary education for only a tiny minority of the population and the inequality of access to secondary schools:

> It is still possible for the largest education authority in the country to propose to erect inequality of educational opportunity into a principle of public policy by solemnly suggesting, with much parade of philosophical arguments, that the interests of the community require that the children of well-to-do parents, who pay fees, should be admitted to public secondary schools on easier intellectual terms than the children of poor parents who can enter them only with free places, and that the children who are so contemptible as to be unable to afford secondary education without assistance in the form of maintenance allowances should not be admitted unless they reach a higher intellectual standard still! (Tawney, 1922).

However, the question of what secondary education for all really meant was neglected: no thought was given to the kind of curriculum which would be suitable, and the seeds of the divisive tripartite system were already present in the Labour Party thinking reflected in this document. For most Labour members at the time 'secondary education for all' did not

mean the same kind of secondary education for all. Rodney
Barker's assessment of Tawney's contribution is as follows:

> His had been one of the most eloquent voices calling for educational
> reform during the war. Education seemed to him one of the most
> important means of creating a sense of community in a nation which
> he felt to be tragically divided. Though he did not himself make any
> new or startling recommendations for educational policy, he seized
> upon the ideas of educationalists and local education authorities and
> gave them highly effective publicity — in his own writings, in the
> columns of the Manchester Guardian . . . and through the Labour
> Party and its advisory committee. Although his dominance in the
> Party's educational councils was declining in the 1930s, his remained
> the major inter-war contribution to the formulation of its educa-
> tional principles (Barker, 1972: 36-37).

In the same chapter, however, Barker goes on to a specific
criticism of *Secondary Education for All:*

> *Secondary Education for All* had two qualities which rendered it an
> almost perfect illustration of the character of the Labour Party
> which produced it. It drew on the concepts of citizenship, common-
> wealth, equality, and social justice, and set the educational system in
> the midst of the struggle to replace a divided materialistic society
> with one properly attuned to intellectual and spiritual values. But its
> proposals were taken directly from the educational system of its
> time and were no more and no less than an extension into general
> practice and at the more generous level of expenditure of particular
> experiments and ideas less well publicised than Tawney's. (p. 43).

In the 1923 election the Conservatives gained the largest
number of seats but lost their overall majority in the House
of Commons. Labour had increased its representation by
nearly 50 and MacDonald was called upon to form a government. The first Labour government lasted less than a year
from January 1924 but it was an important period in the

formation of Labour Party policies. The Party at this time was still largely a working-class party devoted to liberal ideas, and most of the Labour leadership were liberals rather than socialists. C. P. Trevelyan became the President of the Board of Education. Trevelyan, a wealthy landowner whose father was a baronet, had previously been a member of the Liberal Party and a junior minister in the Board of Education in 1908. He resigned from the Liberal Party in 1914, in protest against Britain's entry into the World War, joined the ILP four years later, and became Labour member for Newcastle in 1922. The change of party, however, did not indicate conversion to socialism. There was little possibility of the 1922 Labour policy of 'secondary education for all' being put into operating by Trevelyan even if the finances had been available in 1924.

Prior to the election the Hadow Committee had been set up by the Conservative administration and this was continued by the Labour government. R. H. Tawney was a member of this Committee. (The Labour Party has sometimes been given the credit – doubtful though it is – of setting up the Hadow Committee, but this is incorrect.) Barker (p. 50) points out that one member of the Consultative Committee had stated that

> An enquiry of this kind would be useful in dispelling the socialist and Labour war-cry of 'secondary education for all', and it was important to dispel the notion if possible before the Labour Party came into power. (Board of Education Papers, 24 December 1926, quoted by Barker.)

But Labour in office did not pursue 'secondary education for all' as a policy, and were diverted to trying to establish a better policy for secondary school fees. Trevelyan himself certainly did not believe that it was possible to give all adolescents the same kind of schooling, and agreed that 'there is no question . . . of imposing on all children the kinds of secondary education which are most common today'. (The 'New Direction in Education', *Manchester Guardian,* 6 May 1924, quoted by Barker, p. 54). Unfortunately, Tawney did not suggest what *kind* of secondary education would be suitable for all children either on this occasion or any other. The only difference between the Parties at this stage was on the amount of access to selective education: the Labour and Liberal Parties wanted more access than the Conservatives but they were not now proposing secondary education for all pupils.

When the Labour Party fell in November 1924, Trevelyan appealed for education to be kept out of politics and for all Parties to work for gradual expansion in education. The Conservatives agreed but immediately embarked upon a number of economies which stirred the Labour Party into bitter opposition. At the next Annual Conference (1925) there was a demand for working-class education which would emphasize socialist values, and co-operation rather than competition. This was a refreshing change from having no policy, but it was unfortunately rhetoric — at the level of slogans rather than theory.

The Hadow Report was published in December 1926. The Report was a strange mixture: in some respects pushing the policies for secondary education much further, in other respects making no progress at all and in fact building up troubles for future years. The progress recommended by the Report was that the school leaving age should be raised to 16 within six years, all children should begin secondary school education at 11 (thus getting rid of elementary and making a clean break at 11 from primary to secondary); all pupils would therefore be getting some kind of post-primary education either in grammar schools, central schools or senior

divisions of elementary schools. It was also recommended
that eventually all adolescents should be subject to similar
regulations and thus get equality of provision including staffing. However, the reactionary element of the Report was
that 'all go forward, though along different paths. Selection
by differentiation takes the place of selection by elimination'
(p. 78). This was in fact the beginning of a tripartite policy
which was to delay genuine secondary education for all.

However, the government did not implement the proposal
for raising the school leaving age. Eustace Percy resorted to
the ploy of leaving arrangements to local authorities on the
assumption that most pupils would still leave at 14. Given the
shortage of money at the time, a choice had to be made by
the Conservative administration: either to improve education
(including secondary education) for *all* children, or to put the
available money into selective education for the minority of
able pupils. Eustace Percy took the traditional conservative
line, and for a short time united the Labour Party in opposition to this policy. Trevelyan wrote a letter to *The Times*
opposing Eustace Percy's decision not to raise the school
leaving age; his argument is extremely interesting:

> Set off against this increased expenditure on education would be the
> saving in unemployment benefit and poor relief for the fathers of
> families who are indirectly unemployed because five hundred
> thousand children are annually thrust into the labour market at 14.
> (*The Times,* 10 January 1927, quoted by Barker, p. 58).

A strangely non-educational argument to be employed by
one of the education experts in the Labour Party.

It was also in 1926 that Eustace Percy abolished the
regulations for elementary schools which had laid down the
curriculum requirements which had to be observed in all
state-supported schools. John White has recently (1975) sug-

gested that this was a deliberate attempt to prevent future Labour governments getting control of the school curriculum and using it for political ends. If so it passed unnoticed by the Labour politicians at the time who raised no objection to this removal of regulations.

In the 1929 general election the Labour Party won more seats than any other (287 out of a total of 615) and formed its second minority government. The economic difficulties were probably even greater than in 1924, and education was not a high priority. Trevelyan returned to the Board of Education. He accepted the feeling in the party that the school leaving age should be raised to 15 but at first failed to persuade the Prime Minister and the Cabinet. There was a good deal of pressure in the Party outside Parliament however, and eventually the Prime Minister agreed that a Bill would be introduced to raise the school leaving age to 15 in April 1931. There were problems about maintenance grants as well as difficulties with the Catholic and Church of England schools, however, and the Bill was eventually withdrawn and another Bill introduced which also failed to become law. Trevelyan had resigned in protest at the lack of support for his modest measure, before the Labour Party sank into the chaos of 1931, culminating in the break up of the Party and the MacDonald coalition. Education had not been a high priority during the short life of the second Labour government.

In opposition the Labour Party could once again afford the luxury of slightly more left-wing policies, especially since they had lost at least part of their right-wing into the National government. The National Association of Labour Teachers in 1930 had begun to become a force within the Party. It produced a pamphlet called *Education — A Policy* in which it urged that children over the age of 11 should all be taught in common secondary schools. The argument was put forward that only by having children in one kind of school could genuine equality be promoted. It was proposed that grammar schools and modern schools should be abolished as separate entities and all schools should broaden their curricula. However, the recommendations were too radical for the Labour Party even at the time when they had taken a turn towards the left. Most Labour Party members still thought that progress lay in the direction of improving the conditions of entry for able working-class children to be supported in the grammar school system. Meanwhile, the National government policy was moving in the opposite direction. In 1932 it was proposed, in new regulations, to replace free places in grammar schools by special places. This was a system of fee-paying places according to a means-test of parental income. The Labour Party reacted by seeing this as a direct attack on the opportunities for working-class children to get secondary education. There was considerably more enthusiasm for opposing the kind of change in regulation than there had been to support the positive proposals of the NALT to have a genuine advance in Labour policy in education.

In 1933 the Consultative Committee in Education was asked to enquire into secondary education. It continued to meet between 1933 and November 1938 when the Report (The Spens Report) was published. The NALT during these years took part in the discussions about multibias or multilateral schools and did their best to influence the view of the Consultative Committee on the desirability of the common school idea. The Labour Party as a whole, however, was unenthusiastic about this issue. In 1934 the TUC Conference supported the idea of the common school but the Labour Party in the same year produced a policy document, *Labour and Education,* which completely left out the possibility of common secondary schools, and concentrated on almost nonpartisan topics about fees, special places and the now traditional goal of raising the school leaving age, all of them being differences about 'when?' or 'how much?' rather than any principle.

In London there was a little more progress: the LCC Elementary Education and Higher Education Sub-Committee proposed introducing multilateral non-selective schools in London. But this came to nothing in the thirties partly for administrative reasons (grammar schools and other kinds of post-primary institutions were governed by different sets of regulations still called elementary and secondary). Another difficulty was that even in the 'progressive' LCC there was little real understanding of the comprehensive ideal: the illogical policy developed of planning both common secondary schools and grammar schools in the same areas. That argument is unfortunately still with us now not only as the official Conservative Party programme for secondary education, but also in some Labour thinking.

When the Spens Report was published in 1938, it virtually rejected the idea of multilateral or comprehensive schools and put forward what later became known as the tripartite system. This served to stir one or two Labour Party members into a little more action on secondary education, even if the thinking was still somewhat confused:

> H. B. Lees-Smith, who in 1937 had been calling for variety with equality, condemned a system which 'you would have three types of schools: secondary schools training boys for black-coated occupations; technical high schools in which the boys would be expected to become foremen and technical workers; and then the senior schools, for other jobs which are available'.

W. G. Cove, who had not previously shown any enthusiasm for the multilateral school, declared that the Spens Report conclusion

cannot be sustained on the basis of educational principle and practice; it can only be sustained on the basis of social implication and
social policy. As a matter of fact, I see the multi-lateral schools as a
microcosm of real democracy' (Barker, pp. 72-73).

The Labour Party's Education Advisory Committee once
more took up the idea of the multilateral school as a possible
Labour Party policy. In 1939 it advised Labour MPs and the
TUC that local education authorities should be required to
plan a systematic development of multilateral schools. Multilateral schools did not become official Party policy, but the
Labour Party began, in many localities including the LCC, to
be associated with planning multilateral schools as a practical
way of dealing with the problem of secondary education for
all.
    Support for multilateral schools had not, however, wiped
out the Labour Party's general support for grammar school
education. Still failing to appreciate the essential meaning of
the common school idea, the majority of the Party wanted
the best of both worlds: to extend grammar school provision
for more working-class children and to have multilateral
schools as well. This was sadly still the case when Labour
members became part of the coalition government in May
1940 and began contributing to the general war-time discussions about post-war educational policy which resulted in
the 1943 White Paper and the 1944 Education Act.
    In June 1941 the Board of Education issued a Green Book
as a basis for discussion on the possible reform of education
after the war. Throughout the war the Labour Party failed to
develop a coherent policy for education. Not only were they
confused but they also continued to be internally divided.
Tawney never liked the idea of multilateral schools and his
views were shared by many other prominent Labour educationists, most of whom appeared to regard some kind of

tripartite system as inevitable. In 1942 the TUC came out with a document in support of common schools, but the Labour Party Education Committee was completely divided on this. The meaning of the common or multilateral school was gradually clarified, but when the meaning became clear it was the wrong meaning.

> We believe it is sound that every child in the state should go to the same kind of school. The curriculum will be different and will provide for different aptitudes for varying types of children. (Harold Clay at the Labour Party Annual Conference, quoted by Barker, pp. 77-78.)

Barker goes on to suggest that there were now three opinions on common schools within the Labour Party: first, opposition to them in any form; secondly, support for their introduction as *additions* to the existing system; and thirdly, support for the common school as the only kind of secondary school. It is not clear from Clay's statement which group he belonged to, and this is characteristic of the confusion of the time. What was clear was that many Labour Party politicians saw the comprehensive school not as a way of achieving a common education for all but as a device to improve the efficiency of selection. One argument was that by having children of various abilities under one roof it would be possible to make selection a continuous process without the difficulty of a final choice at the age of 11. The White Paper on education published in July 1943 appeared strongly to favour the tripartite system, mentioning grammar, modern and technical schools as the three main types. In the same year the Committee which had been appointed to enquire into secondary schools' curricula under the chairmanship of Sir Cyril Norwood published its Report just after the publication of the White Paper. The Norwood Report was even more strongly in favour of three kinds of school for three kinds of ability. The coalition government accepted the Norwood recommendations and seemed therefore to support the idea of the tripartite system. But the tripartite system had been justified in the Report on the very doubtful argument that there were three types of children who could be identified by means of psychological tests and who needed quite different types of curricula. Despite the fact that psychologists generally did not agree with this view (see Chapter 3), opinion within the Labour Party was split, and the split continued up to and after the election of 1945. Many who favoured comprehensive schools began to see them as a clear-cut alternative to the tripartite system, but the outright supporters of grammar schools interpreted the 1944 Act as a basis for the tripartite system with possibly a few experiments with multilateral or comprehensive schools. The majority view within the Parliamentary Party was in favour of the tripartite system.

The 1945 election manifesto *Let Us Face The Future* contained no new educational thinking but simply supported the 1944 Education Act which had been largely the work of the Conservative Minister, R. A. Butler. The opportunity to put forward a new policy based on some kind of socialist or social democratic theory of education was completely missed. The result was that after the 1945 election the Labour administration was faced with the impossible task of implementing an Act about which it had not clarified its policy. Despite this some reviewers of the Labour Party's progress have been generous:

> In 1918 English secondary education was wholly elitist, narrowly selective in both social and intellectual terms. In 1944 it appeared to be wholly democratised, catering for all talents and all classes. Therein lies the achievement of the Labour Party (Parkinson, 1970: 35).

I fail to see the 1944 Act in that way. It may have been a great achievement but not for the Labour Party — by way of evidence it is useful to examine how the Act was seen from the Conservative side:

> Conservative M.P.s did not perfunctorily acquiesce in Butler's proposals for educational reform; they applauded the White Paper on Educational Reconstruction and the Education Bill, since those measures incorporated many key Conservative beliefs, notably the belief in the relevance of traditional religious values, the belief in variety and quality rather than 'gross volume', the belief in the desirability of preserving educational privileges and the belief in hierarchy. (H. Kopsch, unpublished PhD, London 1970, quoted by Addison, 1975.)

After the 1945 election the Labour Party had a massive majority and a unique opportunity to promote a new policy in education. Up to this point excuses could be made for the Labour Party. On the one hand the Liberal influence in the twenties and thirties was still strong, and on the other hand, the first two Labour administrations had neither time nor sufficient majority to undertake radical educational reform. No excuse could be made for the years 1945 to 1951, and this is a time of educational disaster for the Labour Party.

Typical of the lack of theory and lack of policy was the handling of the Ministry of Education pamphlet *The Nation's Schools* (May 1945). This pamphlet, which had been drafted before the Labour government took office, had recommended to local education authorities that secondary schools should be organized on a tripartite basis. Despite protests within the Party from those who supported multilateral schools, Ellen Wilkinson, the new Labour Minister of Education, defended the main proposals of the pamphlet even though she eventually agreed (at the June 1947 Conference)

that certain passages should be rewritten. She based her case
on the policy of parity of esteem. Robin Pedley (1969: 37)
has suggested that the Labour Ministers of Education at this
time were no match for Ministry officials who strongly
favoured retaining the grammar schools and preserving their
totally different curriculum from that of modern schools.
This is probably the best example of the absence of theory
producing a lack of policy which resulted in ministers allowing civil servants to carry on with the policy laid down by
previous administrations. Dennis Marsden (1971: 3) in
Fabian Tract 411 has also emphasized the disadvantage en-
tailed in the fact that 'Labour had never passed any major
piece of educational legislation, but has worked within the
blueprints provided by other governments.'

The split within the Labour Party now took an interesting
form. The government's policy was to implement the 1944
Education Act as it was interpreted by officials and in
particular by *The Nation's Schools*. Inside and outside Parliament, however, there were protests, notably from the NALT,
calling for the withdrawal of the pamphlet and a re-interpre-
tation of the Act in a way which would encourage the
development of comprehensive schools. A debate in the
House of Commons was opened by Margaret Herbison in
March 1946, who suggested that the age of 11 was far too
early to make a decision about selecting a child for a specific
kind of education. She suggested that the only fair policy
would be to have a common school until the legal leaving age.
She criticized the idea of parity of prestige as foolish and
unworkable. She was supported in this debate by W. G. Cove,
President of the NALT and a former President of the NUT,
who called for a withdrawal of *The Nation's Schools* and a
rejection of the tripartite system. Barker points out, however
(p. 87) that even the critics' case was an inconsistent one.
Their demand for a common school was not a rejection of

the elitist grammar school tradition but a belief that it should be made more widely available: that is, they were objecting to the section in the pamphlet which discouraged increasing the percentage of pupils who would go to grammar schools or receive a grammar school type of education: 'Why should we deny to our children the chance of having grammar school education?' (W. G. Cove, 1946 Labour Party Conference, quoted by Barker, p. 87).

I am not sure how right Barker is in this respect: certainly there was a good deal of talk about opportunities to take grammar school examinations, and the curriculum most discussed was the grammar school curriculum, but there was also some discussion about access to a *common* curriculum which was certainly not present in the minds of the Labour Ministers. However, Barker may be right in suggesting that Herbison and Cove and other critics had still not fully worked out their plans for multilateral schools and that if they had had their way at the time the result might well have been the streamed comprehensive schools which were produced in London and elsewhere a few years later.

The conventional Labour Party view at this time was that the tripartite system would work provided that the policy of parity of prestige or parity of esteem was adhered to. This was certainly the line taken by Ellen Wilkinson who argued the case for equality plus diversity. She persisted in the naive view that education had to be varied but if equality of facilities and staffing were achieved then there would be no unfairness in the system. This faith in the possibility of administrative arrangements achieving social justice is another characteristic of Labour politicians at this time and later. There seemed to be a belief that if you got the educational finance and the regulations right then equality would automatically follow. There was little realization of the importance of teachers' attitudes in all this and almost no discussion about the content of the curriculum. A familiar argument used at this time was that many successful Labour Party politicians had succeeded by means of grammar schools and that this important route from working-class homes to universities should be kept open at all costs.

The Nation's Schools was not withdrawn, but it was not re-issued. Ellen Wilkinson died in February 1947 and the document prepared by the Ministry of Education officials when she was Minister was issued under the authority of the new Minister, George Tomlinson. This pamphlet *The New Secondary Education* was issued in June 1947. It was more open on the question of comprehensive schools than *The Nation's Schools* but it still very firmly interpreted the 1944 Act along tripartite lines.

> Everyone knows that no two children are alike. Schools must be different too, or the Education Act of 1944 will not achieve success. They must differ in what they teach and how they teach it, just as pupils differ in tastes and abilities. The secondary school system must consequently offer variety in the curriculum and variety in approach suited to the differing aptitudes and abilities and stages of development of the children concerned. Moreover for many years to come the school life of some children will be longer than that of others. Pupils who hope to go on to the University, for example, will naturally remain at school longer than those who aim at being apprenticed at 15 or 16 . . . . Clearly there must be wide variety in the secondary system. Curriculum must be made to fit the child, and not the child the curriculum. The schools must offer individual children who differ widely from one another the kinds of curriculum that will fit them all to live happily and to become useful members of the community *(The New Secondary Education)*.

It is certainly no exaggeration to say that such a document might well have been produced by a Conservative administration at this time. It had nothing in it which showed that it was approved by a Labour government trying to achieve greater social justice in education.

At this stage there was much good will for the comprehensive idea not only within the NUT but within the more conservatively-minded teachers associations such as the Headmistress and Assistant Mistresses. By 1948, however, the feeling was less optimistic. Owing to the lack of any decisive policy on comprehensive schools suspicion about their respectability was growing within the profession. In 1948 a large majority at the Annual Conference of the NUT refused to condemn the tripartite principle (Banks, 1955: 143). There was a feeling that comprehensive schools were experimental and unproved and there was already a swing back to the idea that the best kind of school was a grammar school, and that children would get only second best education in a comprehensive school. Because of its lack of policy on comprehensive education and the purpose of schooling for *all* children, the Labour Party had effectively missed the boat. When the Labour Party adopted the idea of comprehensive education as official policy in 1951 it was already in many respects too late. The general election in 1950 had reduced the Labour majority drastically and Atlee's new government seemed to be tired and lacking in vision. When the Conservative administration took over in the following year the Labour Party was still by no means united although Party policy had changed in favour of comprehensive schools. Tomlinson, the Minister of Education, had clearly never understood the issues and had played the safe game of preserving the prestige of grammar schools. He even boasted of his 'neutrality' on the comprehensive school issue, which really meant he had resisted change as much as possible.

The Party left office with its attitudes to comprehensive education unclear. Official Party policy, on the other hand, appeared a little more certain . . . The last years of Labour office had been critical for the Minister of Education as both the mass movement and then the NEC itself moved to oppose ministerial policy of only limited experiment for the comprehensive schools. The shift in opinion was finally marked by the publication in 1951 of *Secondary Education For All.* That document committed the Party to a policy of comprehensive reorganisation. There was little attention paid to the issue in the immediate period after Labour left office. It had not at that time become a feature of Party conflict, and education generally fell into the backwaters of daily politics (Parkinson, 1970: p. 71).

In opposition there was little more discussion about what comprehensive education meant. The NEC seemed to favour a system of junior and senior comprehensive schools rather than the large London comprehensives, 11-18, which were proving difficult to administer, but the debate centred on organization and administration rather than on social and educational principles. How could it have been otherwise when no one appeared to have a theory of education – only negative arguments against selection and the tripartite system? These arguments were getting better, supported as they were by growing quantities of sociological and psychological evidence, but it was still negative: no one appeared to be discussing the meaning of real secondary education for all or how common schools might achieve these aims.

In 1954 Margaret Cole made a noble effort to sort out some of the confusion in *What is a Comprehensive School?* She also appealed for Party unity in this document, but the discussion was again at the level of immediate tactics rather than long-term policy based on socialist principles. After losing the 1955 election another Labour policy document was produced in 1956 *(Towards Equality)* which was strong on the arguments against injustice in society such as the evils of the tripartite system, but weak on a positive policy for education. In the same year (1956) Anthony Crosland's book

The Future of Socialism was published: of its 529 pages 20 were devoted to a chapter on education, but these were much weaker in tone and in content than most of the rest of the book. The chapter is limited to common sense remarks about the contribution of education to inequality — especially the public schools — and a few defensive arguments against the attack made on comprehensive schools by Eric James (who even then hardly deserved so much attention), and finally a few proposals for the cautious development of the comprehensive pattern throughout the country. His argument was basically that 'The school system in Britain remains the most divisive, unjust, and wasteful of all the aspects of social inequality' (Crosland, 1956: 258). But there was no new educational theory in the book and no discussion of the educational theories of others. I do not wish to cast too much blame on Crosland for this: I am merely pointing out the fact that so little attention was paid to education, and suggesting that one reason for this is that educational theory is much more difficult to indulge in than is generally realized by Labour politicians. Conservative politicians are in this respect luckier — they have no need of a theory to preserve the status quo or move backwards a little!

More serious is Crosland's attempt to elevate common sense to the level of educational theory:

> But both common sense and American experience suggest that this (ie non-streaming) would lead to a really serious levelling down of standards, and a quite excessive handicap to the clever child. Division into streams, according to ability, remains essential (p. 272).

Confusion within the Party continued throughout the 1950s. The meaning of comprehensive was still unclear despite Margaret Cole's attempt. The majority of comprehensive schools which had been established were really tripartite systems under one roof. In London, for example, the policy was to 'stream like mad' (Pedley, 1969: 68). The majority of Labour MPs still seemed to favour this kind of meritocracy in education even when they spoke of equality. Michael Young's book *The Rise of Meritocracy* (1958) should have been the final nail in the coffin of grammar schools and the meritocratic position, but it had little effect. In 1959, Roy Jenkins published *The Labour Case* in which he argued that grammar schools should be preserved and comprehensive schools should merely fill in the gaps in a developing system.

Even *Learning to Live* (published by the Labour Party in June 1958), although it appeared to be whole-heartedly in favour of comprehensive schools, failed to reject the discredited psychological view that there were different 'types' of child needing different types of education — grammar, technical or modern (p. 28).

In 1964 a Labour government was elected and Anthony Crosland was put in charge of education. A year later he issued the now famous Circular 10/65 which requested (but did not require) LEAs to submit plans for comprehensive reorganization. The Circular itself is more notable for its definition of acceptable patterns of comprehensive organization than for any contribution it made to comprehensive school policy. It was also found to be not much use in forcing the hand of Conservative-controlled authorities, so in the following year a stronger Circular 10/66 was issued threatening that funds would be withheld from tardy authorities. This may have speeded up the development of comprehensive schools to some extent, but it was an empty half-victory. On the one hand there was still no clear theory about the purpose of secondary education, and on the other hand the DES officials seemed to want to anaesthetize the process as much as possible.

A lack of central guidance and definition appears clearly from the form of circular 10/65 itself. No commitment was made to comprehensive reorganisation, the Circular merely commenting on six schemes which had been tried out by local authorities. Some of the schemes were not even comprehensive in that they retained parental 'choice' of transfer into an academic sector, a choice exercised mainly by middle class parents. Middle schools, the one scheme which was feasible without rebuilding, were at first explicitly discouraged (although this injunction was later withdrawn). Throughout, the civil servants behaved as if there were no controversy. It has been pointed out that certain actions of the new Department of Education and Science seemed to assume the permanent co-existence of comprehensives with the bipartite structure (Marsden, Fabian Tract 411, 1971: 16).

The circulars were of course withdrawn by Mrs Thatcher in 1970, but the requirement was repeated by the next Labour government, and finally acquired the force of law by the 1976 Act. The outstanding need now is still that the purpose of comprehensive schools should be clarified — not least for the benefit of pupils' parents. And this can only be achieved, as I suggested in Chapter 1, in terms of a statement about a common curriculum, that is, what any child in our society needs to have as basic curriculum content. One of the advantages of grammar schools has been that they have had a policy on curriculum. Even if it was a very unsatisfactory curriculum in many respects it had a clear structure and tradition. For this reason Prime Minister Callaghan's 1976 call for a national debate on education was welcome, even if it originally appeared to be based on a rather doubtful policy of making schools subservient to the needs of society, and even if the secret Yellow Paper on which his speech was based betrayed many of the DES officials' familiar attitudes and prejudices in education, as well as a number of factual errors.

In order to play a better game against the professional administrators it will be increasingly necessary for Labour politicians to operate more efficiently at two different levels. The first is to clarify fundamental principles within the Party about society and education; the second to do their homework more carefully on important questions of detail in education. I should like to illustrate this problem of detail by referring to one particular issue which came to a head in the latter part of 1976: the question of school examinations at age 16. The issues are, as usual, extremely complex but at the risk of over-simplification I will try to keep the outline as brief as possible.

Since 1951 grammar school pupils have taken the General Certificate of Education Ordinary (GCE 'O') level at 16. Secondary modern pupils were originally intended to be spared the delights of examinations altogether, but eventually, partly due to the inevitable errors of selection, partly due to the pressure from parents and employers, the more 'academic' pupils from secondary modern schools were entered for GCE 'O' level in ever increasing numbers. Other pupils were entered for a variety of examinations, most of them quite unsuitable for 16-year-olds. The Beloe Committee was set up to look into this problem, and when it reported in 1960 it recommended that there should be a new examination for the ability range covering roughly the next 40 percent below the top 20 percent who took GCE 'O' level. Thus, a new form of tripartite categorization was created for so-called comprehensive schools: GCE for the academic top 20 percent, CSE for the next 40 percent, and no form of assessment for the bottom 40 percent – the non-examinables. By 1976 the point at issue was this: many comprehensive schools have tried to delay selection as long as possible by abolishing rigid streaming in all subjects and introducing more flexible methods of grouping such as 'setting' for a few subjects; a small number of schools have even established a common curriculum policy for the whole range of pupils on the argument that equal opportunity in education means equal access to knowledge; some have compulsory elements for all pupils covering such subjects as Mathematics, English and Science. Such policies work well until about the age of 14 when examinations have to be considered. In one way or another pupils have to be segregated and prepared for GCE or CSE (some schools just ignore the 20 + 40 percent guidelines and enter all pupils for an examination). But the necessity of having to work with two Examination Boards, two sets of syllabus, etc. is not only a nuisance to teachers it also inhibits their developing a genuinely common curriculum for the whole range of abilities.

Several years ago the Schools Council was asked to tackle this problem. It has tried out common examinations at 16+ in a number of subjects and as a result of these trials, in July 1976 the Schools Council recommended that a common system at 16+ should be adopted in the 1980s. The DES officials have opposed the new common examination, for financial and administrative reasons, and the new Secretary of State for Education, Mrs Shirley Williams, took their advice — apparently with some reluctance. Further delays will now be inevitable and the move towards genuine comprehensive schools made much more difficult. The point about all this is not to criticize the Secretary of State, who was faced with a difficult decision immediately on taking office, but to point out that very little interest was aroused by this decision both inside and outside Parliament. For most it was presumably a boring detail about examination administration: in fact very important principles were involved which affect general policy on comprehensive education. The Labour Party, having no real policy, were yet again at the mercy of civil servants who tend to be both over-cautious and out of date.

In this chapter I have concentrated on the lack of educational theory particularly concerning comprehensive schools. This is where lack of theory is most serious, but there are other problem areas as well — primary schools, the 16-19 age group and adult education, for example. We are in danger of falling behind European thinking on 'recurrent education' and 'permanent education'. In addition the problem of public schools remains unsolved. What price social justice when privilege in education can be purchased for about £1200 a year? On this topic Parkinson (1970), a generally very sympathetic observer of the Labour Party, is critical:

> It is probably fair to say that the Party . . . has underestimated the need for an attack on the problems of social and educational privilege exhibited by those schools. Arguably, the issue was as much a challenge to its idealism as was tripartism, and the need for consistency alone would probably demand some radical action (p. 126).

Parkinson follows this with a more general criticism:

> The Party has not shown a sufficient understanding of the sociological aspects of educational change, and has thought too much in terms of legislative and administrative change (p. 126).

There has certainly been an exaggerated belief in the power of legislation and administrative machinery, but I would not entirely agree that the major area of neglect is sociological. It seems to me that the whole field of educational theory is the weakness; philosophical and psychological studies have been insufficiently taken into account, and more recently curriculum theory has been almost completely ignored.

8

NOTES TOWARDS A THEORY
OF DEMOCRATIC
EDUCATIONAL PLANNING

INTRODUCTION

In previous chapters I have been extremely critical of certain well-established points of view in education and I feel that I ought to end the book on a more positive and constructive note. On the other hand it might seem very presumptuous to put forward a theory for educational planning in a society as complex and so rapidly changing as ours. I would like to make it clear that I am putting forward certain views as a basis for discussion rather than any kind of final programme. But it does seem to me to be very important, indeed quite essential, that decision-making in education should rest on a better basis of theory than has been the case in the past. The focus of the debate so far has centred on secondary schools, and in particular the central problem of comprehensive education. Although there are other problems equally important in education at the moment, I have chosen to concentrate on the comprehensive issue since it is a crucial stage in educational planning, and also because it does illustrate in many respects the whole problem of attitudes to education and educational planning. It is also important because at this point in time the comprehensive issue has reached a critical stage in its exemplification of the problem of social justice in education.

We might say that the first stage of this process was during the 1920s and 1930s when there was some pressure to achieve greater *access* to secondary education for larger numbers of working-class pupils — this was seen as the central problem of equality or social justice in those days. The second stage would cover roughly the 1940s and 1950s. This was the time of growth of secondary education *for all* but in the diluted form of a tripartite system. We have seen that it was then gradually realized that the tripartite system was unworkable as well as unjust. The tripartite system also became the bipartite system, with grammar schools for roughly the top 20 percent of the ability range and secondary modern schools for the rest who were labelled as non-academic or less able. The policy of parity of prestige or parity of esteem was never realistic in a society where differences in prestige were so closely connected with occupation, and occupational placement was so closely connected with educational achievement. The third stage of the story roughly covered the 1960s. By then the growth of comprehensive schools theoretically presented equal educational opportunity or equally fair chances for all pupils, but Julienne Ford (1969) and others soon pointed out that if comprehensive schools simply operated a tripartite system under one roof, very little was gained by abolishing selection at 11+. Finally, the fourth stage: in the 1970s, there was an increase in interest in questions about the curriculum. Those teachers who did not accept the idea that a comprehensive school should be no more than a tripartite system under one roof were forced to ask such questions as 'What is the point of common schools without a common curriculum?' and 'How can we have genuine comprehensive education unless schools transmit a common culture?'. In other words, we are now seeing a change of emphasis from structure and organization of comprehensive schools to an analysis of the content of the curriculum. Previously comprehensive schools had tended to operate with a watered-down version of a grammar school curriculum or an uneasy amalgamation of elementary and grammar curricula. Until very recently few comprehensive schools had thought out their curriculum from first principles. In 1976 this discussion of the curriculum began to reach an important point for decision-making. Schools, including comprehensive schools, were under attack, and in particular there were suggestions that standards were falling or at least failing to rise sufficiently. Accountability was very much in the air, and for the last few years the Department of Education and Science has had an Assessment of Performance Unit (APU) which is planning to monitor standards or at least to provide a means for checking on certain kinds of educational development.

At earlier stages in the progress towards comprehensive schools we have seen that the Labour Party was severely handicapped by its lack of educational theory. Now educational theory is absolutely crucial: partly to deal with the problem of curriculum planning in general, and partly to deal with questions of evaluation and standards. One of the problems that the APU has already discovered is that it is no use assessing something without first of all establishing that it has a rightful place in the curriculum. Certainly one of the weaknesses of much educational assessment in the US (and rumour has it that American standards have influenced the thinking of the APU to a great extent) is that they operate with a very inadequate model of education. This is not surprising because, as I have stressed a number of times throughout this book, educational theory is extremely difficult. This accounts for the fact that some educational theory in the past has been very bad and sometimes very boring, but it is very necessary all the same. In addition the most difficult aspect of education theory is that part of it which deals with the content of education — recently referred to as curriculum theory. Because curriculum theory is extremely complex and extremely difficult there has been a tendency for education decision-makers to retreat to questions of organization and administration, and for education theorists to retreat into separate respectable disciplines, so that we have very high quality philosophy of education, sociology of education and psychology, but much less respectable theory at the level of curriculum decision-making. But if we are not to allow politicians and educational administrators to stagger on by trial and error, and probably fall into some very nasty pits on the way, it is essential to develop some kind of theoretical framework which would provide a basis at least for discussion, if not for decision-making.

What then would a socialist or social democratic theory of education look like? Certainly it need not be a 'Utopian' Marxist theory, and it need not be a kind of exercise in futurology (except in the very limited sense used by Halsey in his excellent book *Educational Priority*):

> Goldthorpe distinguishes between futurology as *prediction* and futurology as *design*. Conventional futurology is essentially extrapolation to the future of trends from the recent past. It therefore tends to carry with it the value assumptions of the status quo and is in that sense conservative ... Futurology as *design* is quite another matter and not only because it is inherently more radical in its political possibilities. It is scientifically much more challenging in that it directly requires the social scientist to state clearly what he knows or does not know about the possibility of moving from the

present state to a postulated, presumably desired, future state (Halsey, 1972: 4).

Education theory is therefore an elucidation of the values in order to guide action in a desirable direction.

The very idea of an educational theory is itself an arena of conflict in the world of philosophy of education. I will not attempt to summarize the controversy here: T. W. Moore (1974) has neatly outlined the arguments and put forward his own views on the necessity for theory in the way that he defines it. Moore suggests that an educational theory tries to give 'comprehensive, over-arching guidance in the conduct of education . . . usually associated with a distinctive social and political position' (Moore, 1974: 8-9). An educationl theory, is therefore essentially *prescriptive,* unlike scientific theory, and any attempt to keep educational theory out of politics is doomed to failure. Any of the well-known theorists of educa- tion — Plato, Rousseau or Dewey — had a particular political axe to grind. Whether you want to change society in a particular way or leave it as it is, this is a political stance; whether you want to educate *all* people or only *some* of them is a reflection of social and political values.

Moore suggests that any general educational theory must rest on three kinds of assumptions or value-judgements:

(1) assumptions about those who are to be educated — human beings and especially children;

(2) assumptions about the purpose or *aims* of education; and

(3) assumptions about the nature of *knowledge,* especially the worthwhileness of certain kinds of knowledge. Assump- tions about knowledge will usually include assumptions about how knowledge is acquired and therefore how it is learnt and should be taught.

For example, in England probably the most influential

educational theory in the nineteenth century was the Utilitarian theory associated with Jeremy Bentham, James Mill and his son John Stuart Mill (who introduced some important reservations into the theory having experienced it himself as a child). In its 'pure' form as written by James Mill (1821) the theory rests on the following three sets of assumptions:

1. About the nature of man.
    1.1. Human beings are essentially selfish. Men (and children) act only to increase pleasure or to avoid pain. (The Utilitarian doctrine of psychological hedonism.)
    1.2. Human beings at birth are intellectually empty. Their minds are, initially, like clean slates or empty rooms gradually to be filled up with the furniture provided by experiences from sensations derived from the environment. Moore reminds us that Mr Gradgrind in Dickens's novel exemplified Utilitarian theory by regarding his job as filling children up with facts, and this aspect of Utilitarian theory has by no means disappeared today.

2. Assumptions about aims (or the educated man).
    2.1. The purpose of all rational activity (including education) is to increase happiness and diminish pain.
    2.2. The particular aim of education is to produce the kind of man whose behaviour will increase not only his own happiness but also that of other human beings.
    2.3. The educated man would have virtues of temperance, generosity and justice together with useful knowledge and sagacity (that is the ability to use knowledge wisely).

3. Assumptions about knowledge and pedagogy.
    3.1. Connected with the clean slate theory of mind (1.2 above) was the doctrine that ideas tend to associate to-

gether according to the frequency with which elements in the environment are experienced together (e.g. fire and heat are natural connections of this kind, but society also tries to build up 'social' connections between stealing and punishment, etc.)

3.2. Education consists of forming in pupils' minds desirable trains of ideas.

3.3. The curriculum should consist of associations of the natural kind as well as the artificial — science and mathematics as well as history, literature, philosophy and religion.

3.4. Effective method would be the systematic joining of certain sensations and ideas in the pupil by presenting them frequently and in the context of pleasure.

This is a very sketchy and inadequate account of James Mill's theory of education. Those interested in a fuller version, together with criticisms of it, should read Moore (1974) or Burston (1969). Meanwhile, Moore's summary will suffice (p. 41):

> Granted the need to produce an individual who, not withstanding his natural egoism, is to be a means to the general happiness, then, by an appropriate arrangement of his experiences, associate in his mind those ideas which are the basis of desirable actions. Such associations will constitute the knowledge, the skills and the attitudes which will enable him to take his place in social life. The pressure of social approval or disapproval, by increasing or decreasing his own happiness, will prompt him to play his part well.

I will not attempt a detailed criticism of this theory here but will merely indicate a few of the assumptions on which a twentieth-century socialist or social democrat might disagree with a nineteenth-century Utilitarian. It may be worth noting that this disagreement will be partly a question of value-judgements but partly also a question of knowledge: since James Mill we have, for example, gained a good deal more scientific evidence about the nature of human beings and their learning processes.

(1) On the nature of man, it is no longer generally assumed that man is essentially a selfish egoist. Most of us now would think that this is only a partial truth. James Mill tended to play down the fact that man is essentially a social being, not necessarily a selfish individualist all the time. In order to explain non-selfish behaviour Utilitarians have to resort to very complicated arguments. We would now tend to suggest that James Mill was likely to have been prejudiced by the prevailing individualistic philosophy of his day and to ignore the fact that man's progress has been due mainly to co-operation and communal effort rather than individualistic achievements. It is even more disputed now that the infant mind is a tabula rasa or clean slate. Some, like Chomsky, insist on innate 'deep structures' which channel development (especially language) but we would still probably accept the very great importance of environment. However, 'filling up with facts' is now definitely out of favour − learning principles and generalizations is much more important, and therefore we need to structure the environment carefully to ensure this (a point often forgotten by the naive progressivists who would allow the child simply to learn from experience).

(2) Assumptions about aims. At this level there is probably a good deal of agreement between the twentieth-century socialist and a nineteenth-century Utilitarian. This is where the Labour Party and others took over Utilitarian philosophy via liberal politics (and perhaps common sense). The main difference would, however, be the change of emphasis from the *individual* to *society* as a whole. Another

important difference is that Utilitarian philosophy assumed that people ought to be educated, in the main, for their status in life; mobility should be encouraged up to a point, but too much mobility would be disruptive. Socialist thinking would therefore place much more emphasis on the question of social justice than the Utilitarians in this particular respect.

(3) Assumptions about knowledge and pedagogy. Our view of worthwhile knowledge would certainly be different from the kind of curriculum that James Mill set out for his son, John Stuart Mill (who learnt Greek at the age of 4). Nevertheless, we are still to some extent in the Utilitarian tradition of knowledge and worthwhileness, but there is probably more disagreement at the level of psychology of learning. The greatest need now is for much more careful work on the justification of certain kinds of knowledge. Although James Mill wrote a great deal about the acquisition of knowledge, he spent much less time justifying his particular selection from the culture.

This now leaves the way clear to outline a socialist theory of education. I want to stress immediately how difficult this is, and that I am only putting forward a few suggestions as a basis for discussion, rather than a definitive version of what a theory would be or what policies should be adopted.

(1) Assumptions about the nature of man.

1.1. Men are not essentially selfish. Nor are they essentially good (as Rousseau and the naive progressivists supposed). They are a mixture of potentialities good and evil.

1.2. Children are naturally curious; they want to learn. But curiosity will not necessarily carry them all the way that is necessary in a modern complex society. There will still be a need to develop some of the Utilitarian values such as hard work, perseverance, etc.

1.3. Man is essentially a social being. This should be reflected both in *what* is learnt and *how* it is learnt.

1.4. All can benefit from education (no one is ineducable). Although socialists tend to think that environment is very important and will be sceptical of intelligence tests, this does not mean that we think that everyone is equally intelligent. Some will learn more than others but this is essentially a difference in degree rather than a difference in kind. Whereas some theories of education emphasize differences, a socialist theory of education will emphasize the essential humanity of all human beings.

(2) Aims. (Education is concerned with improving or developing people in some way.)

2.1. In a democratic society is is necessary for individuals to become autonomous, that is, to be able to make decisions for themselves over a wide range of activities rather than to do just as they are told.

2.2. But the aim will be to produce not simply an autonomous individual but an autonomous individual living in society knowing his duties and responsibilities as well as his rights and privileges. The educated man in a democratic society is a co-operative individual not a selfish individualist.

2.3 The aim will be to introduce *all* members of society to the common culture of that society. It will not be enough to succeed with a small minority, and it will not be satisfactory to have a different kind of education for different social or intellectual levels. Social justice in education must mean equality of access to worthwhile knowledge and experience (although accepting and welcoming different levels of achievement in different kinds of knowledge).

(3) Assumptions about knowledge and pedagogy.

3.1. There is no particular socialist theory of the structure of knowledge (this is a technical question of epistemology about which socialists have no particular insights).

3.2. But it is possible to value some kinds of knowledge more highly than others. Those kinds of knowledge and experiences will be valued in so far as they contribute to the aims of education.

3.3. It will be necessary for socialists to make problems of educational knowledge rather than to take them for granted. That is, we must be careful not to assume that the traditional allocation of knowledge in the curriculum is a good one, but must subject it to scrutiny in the light of our aims in education, as well as in the light of current philosophical and sociological thinking about the nature of knowledge. This is the most difficult aspect of educational theory and will be dealt with again later in this chapter.

At this point it is necessary to use this basic framework to construct a more definite set of policies for education. In other words to convert theory into practice. I have suggested elsewhere (1973; 1975) that a relatively value-free definition of curriculum is to see it as a selection from the culture of society. If culture is defined as everything man-made in society, then schools have the task of selecting from everything that exists in a particular society (in our case fish and chips and bingo and pop music as well as mathematics, science, art and literature) and deciding that some aspects of our heritage are too important to be left to chance transmission. This has of course been made explicit by other writers on curriculum, for example, Dewey in *Democracy and Education:*

Every society gets encumbered with what is trivial. . . . with what is
positively perverse. The school has the duty of omitting such things
from the environment which it supplies and thereby doing what it
can to counteract their influence in the ordinary social environment.
By selecting the best for its exclusive use, it strives to reinforce the
power of this best. As a society becomes more enlightened, it realises
that it is responsible not to transmit and conserve the whole of its
existing achievements, but only such as make for a better future
society. The school is its chief agency for the accomplishment of this
end.

This is clearly a very important task for those connected with
education decision-making, and curriculum planning in
particular: what knowledge and experiences to include, what
to leave to chance. And, further sub-dividing this, what
knowledge and experiences to include as absolutely essential
for *everyone*, and what can be left as minority tastes.

At this stage it is necessary to point out an important
paradox in education: if our aim is to produce autonomous
individuals to what extent is this possible by compelling
children to go to schools and compelling them to undergo
certain experiences within those schools? Seen in a different
way the problem might be presented thus: compulsory
schooling deprives young people of eleven years' 'freedom';
in a democratic society if we compel anyone to do anything
we should have good reasons to justify it. So if we compel
children to go to school for eleven years we should be able to
say in what ways we *hope* they will be improved. This
improvement will be partly a matter of skills and attitude but
it is a mistake to ignore content. (One of the misleading
cliches of primary education is to say that children are there
to learn how to learn — which is meaningless unless we know
something about *what* they learn how to learn.) There can be
no guarantees in this of course — education cannot be re-

duced, as some US curriculum theorists used to believe, to a list of behavioural objectives. But if there can be no guarantees, there ought to be meaningful guide-lines and explanations for compulsory education, justifications for any compulsory elements, and some means of pupils knowing the extent to which they are living up to expectations. Most of this is noticeably lacking in many schools today. It is difficult to see how schools could be complete democracies, but what is more worrying is the fact that many schools do not seem even to be part of a democratic society.

We need some way of classifying knowledge and experience to enable educationists to draw up a list of priorities. It is possible for philosophers to produce criteria to judge whether particular kinds of knowledge and kinds of experience are worthwhile in a fairly abstract sense (see Peters, 1966). It is also necessary to say that in our kind of society that there are particular kinds of knowledge which are especially important. This relates to the overriding aim of producing autonomous individuals in society. It is necessary to know what kinds of things would be worthwhile in any society, but also what kinds of activities are particularly necessary to understand and exert mastery over our twentieth-century society. So we might argue, for example, that science is not only worthwhile as a form of knowledge in Professor Peter's sense (being an open-ended activity so that we can never know all there is to know about science, etc.), but we can also say that in modern twentieth-century Britain it is especially important to have some acquaintance with science because without it one cannot participate in democratic procedures and decision-making about such every-day events as conservation and pollution. Therefore we could put up a very good argument for science being placed high on our list of knowledge priorities on grounds of worthwhileness and relevance.

There is, however, another criterion, namely to what extent is it necessary for this knowledge to be taught *in schools* in order for it to be learnt? It is quite feasible that there are certain kinds of very important knowledge which are picked up automatically without it being necessary for schools to concern themselves with it. We might argue, for instance, that it is highly desirable that young people in our society acquire a certain expertise in car driving. Most people will drive cars, and in order to drive safely for their own benefit and for the benefit of society at large they should learn how to do this properly. There is, however, no particular reason why this should be done in schools. There are other agencies outside schools which can cope with this extremely well, and it comes at a stage in life when most young people have left school. Therefore although a case might be made for car driving in schools it would appear to have a lower priority than much more fundamental skills and kinds of knowledge with which the school has particular responsibility and expertise.

We might therefore end up with a very crude two-dimensional model for allocating priorities to certain kinds of activity (Figure 2).

(1) We have already said that science would be rated very high for reasons already given on the worthwhileness and relevance (W.R.) scale and it would also be rated high on the school necessity scale. Science is the kind of knowledge which simply cannot be picked up by chance. By its very nature science is different from common sense. If appearance were the same as reality it would not be necessary for us to have science. Therefore we would give science a very high priority indeed and it would come close to the top and close to the left-hand corner of the box.

(2) Car driving as we have already said, is high in relevance (maybe slightly lower in worthwhileness but that is arguable)

Figure 2

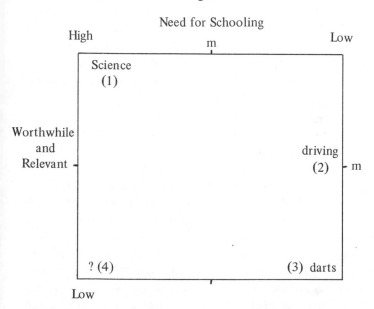

Need for Schooling

High   m   Low

Science (1)

Worthwhile and Relevant

driving (2) — m

? (4)   (3) darts

Low

but it is certainly less necessary for the school to be involved in this. Therefore we would place car driving fairly high on the W.R. scale but on the low (right-hand side) of the school necessity scale.

(3) Playing darts may be an enjoyable activity but hardly an essential aspect of our culture. We would therefore place it low on the W.R. scale and also low on the school necessity scale. Even if it were thought a highly aesthetic activity those who enjoy playing darts apparently find very little difficulty in picking up the necessary skills outside school. There would be little argument therefore in including it in the general curriculum.

(4) Is almost a non-category. This supposes that there could be some kinds of activity which are low on worthwhile-

ness and relevance but high in being necessarily taught by the school. It is not entirely without relevance, however, because many obsolete skills are taught by schools: some would say long-division in mathematics, for example, others might give as examples some kinds of home economics teaching such as how to starch table napkins when this has ceased to be a skill required by most people in our society.

The above is a possible procedure which could be practised at a number of levels in curriculum planning. At the highest possible level of decision-making, nationally, as well as by every teacher and every group of teachers working together. Let us suppose that this kind of activity has taken place and let us make a guess at the kind of list of priorities this might give us. It is almost certain that we could say that, except for a few extremists discussed in earlier chapters, everyone in education would agree that literacy is a desirable aim for everyone. This would be a satisfactory aim for young children in primary schools, but by the age of 10 or 11, and certainly by the age of 13 or 14, we should not only be able to say that children should be able to read and write at a certain rate and with a certain vocabulary, we should also be able to specify *what* they should be able to read. It is a very different matter being able to read a chapter in a history text book and an article in *New Scientist.* Bearing in mind our two-dimensional model, then, I think we might agree on the following kind of list of high priorities in literacy:

Scientific,
Mathematical,
Humanities and social science (including political, economic and social literacy), and
Artistic appreciation and active experience.

We are immediately in some difficulties, because we are now dealing with different *kinds* of desirable experiences and activities. We want to say that we require scientific and mathematical literacy because we are members of a technological scientific society, etc. We can advance the same kinds of arguments for wanting a knowledge of history, and political and economic literacy, i.e. we live in a highly *social* scientific society. But that is not the end of the story: one of the qualifications that John Stuart Mill made about his own education was that it neglected the whole area of *feeling*, and we want an element in the curriculum which encourages creative and expressive work in the Arts because man is that kind of animal — he is unique among other animals in being creative.

This takes us from the purely theoretical level to its practical implications in curriculum planning. We have to say immediately that there is no total agreement on these matters, and secondly that much in the last resort will be left to the teachers themselves; but because there is no total agreement it is all the more necessary to try and reach as much consensus as possible. In a democracy there needs to be a number of levels of curriculum planning. I will restrict discussion at this stage to three levels (bearing in mind that there may be others, and I am sure that representatives of local education authorities will say that they ought to be involved rather than relegated to the side-lines in this respect).

The first level I would suggest is that of *national* curriculum planning. Here we could be satisfied with minimum *guide-lines* such as the four headings I suggested above or maybe the six kinds of development in which the APU have already expressed an interest and an intention to develop tests.

The second level of curriculum development will be that of the *school*. There is in a democracy much greater need for teachers to discuss the school curriculum with parents, with pupils themselves, with governors (as well as to discuss the whole curriculum of the school amongst themselves to a much greater extent than is common). This would be much in keeping with the idea of the educational *covenant* or contract which was proposed by the Schools Council Working Paper No. 53, *The Whole Curriculum 13 to 16.* Teachers are the experts in curriculum planning (or should be) but they have not a monopoly of wisdom; they ought to be able to present an outline as a basis for negotiation, bearing in mind that no matter how desirable they think certain activities are that ultimately pupils will, whether we like it or not, accept or reject the arguments put forward by teachers, and if they reject there is little teachers can do about it. Teachers can persuade but they cannot compel.

The third level of curriculum planning is at the level of the *teacher.* Here he will be concerned with the lesson, the work scheme, the *teaching syllabus.* Ultimately most power will be left in the hands of the individual teacher. He will interpret the minimum guide-lines laid down nationally, he will interpret the general curriculum policy laid down by the school and will teach it in the way that he feels is best. This is inevitable, but what I am suggesting is that this process needs to be made much more open.

Such a scheme ought to avoid the unnecessary squabble over teacher autonomy and the need for national curriculum planning. Two more points need to be made here: the first is that teachers are by no means as free as has sometimes been pretended; they are subject to all sorts of constraints, and it would be better if we were honest about this rather than hypocritically pretending that teachers have much more freedom than they have. The second point is that teacher autonomy should not mean that teachers have a perfect right to do anything that they feel that they would like to do in the classroom (*The Prime of Miss Jean Brodie* is a good cautionary tale here). Teacher autonomy surely implies some kind of corporate responsibility, not the right of any individual to inflict his own idiosyncratic tastes on unwilling pupils.

Finally, we need to consider the question of evaluation, again at the three levels mentioned above: national, school and classroom. A good deal *more* evaluation is necessary at all stages. At the national level we have already mentioned the activities of the APU. I see nothing professionally objectionable in these activities provided they are watched very carefully. There is a considerable need for officials to be guided away from foolish American practices such as placing too much reliance on behavioural objectives. There is also a need to avoid reverting to out-dated ideas about standards although real questions of standards are very important. The other aspect of national monitoring are public examinations, especially those at 16+, eventually we hope a common examination at 16+. This should certainly be a high priority in the future years. At the school level there is an overlap between national monitoring of 16+ examinations and much more use of school-based examinations such as CSE Mode IIIs. It does seem particularly useful to have school-based examinations which are externally moderated and therefore preserving a link between levels I and II.

It should also be recognized that just as the school has a responsibility for the *whole* curriculum, and that the whole curriculum should be more than just a collection of bits and pieces, that also the school as a whole has a responsibility for failure. If a particular teacher fails with a particular group of pupils, this is not just his responsibility, it is the responsibility of the whole school. At the level of the teacher in the classroom, it is much more necessary for teachers to evaluate and keep more careful records of continuous assessment. There is far too little teacher evaluation on a day-to-day basis. Secondly, at the classroom level there is plenty of scope today for self-evaluation of various kinds. Recently many kinds of techniques have been developed for teachers to evaluate their own performance in classrooms. These have been pioneered by University of East Anglia staff members originally on such projects as Safari and the Ford Teaching Project (now transferred to the Cambridge Institute of Education). These are essentially devices for encouraging teachers to re-think their attitudes and to evaluate their own performance in the classroom. This development needs to be made much more available and could be one of the developments in in-service training.

At each of these three levels it will be necessary clearly to differentiate between the common core curriculum and peripheral optional courses for minority tastes. In many schools there is far too much compulsion and at the same time far too little planning and justification for compulsory activities. Some schools, for example, makes games compulsory for all pupils, but allow many to drop science at the age of 13. How can this be justified? Schools need a clear policy on what is core and what is peripheral. They will inevitably be guided to some extent by national statements about curriculum: at present the APU is working in six areas of human development and when these six kinds of development get known by schools (and even more when tests begin to appear) this will indicate certain kinds of priority to the schools. In this respect it is useful for the APU to test *development* rather than curriculum attainment (if that distinction is really possible). This will leave the schools free to teach what they want, to some extent. But there is of course a need for much clearer justification for selecting these six kinds of development than has appeared in any publication so far.

There is also a need for the curriculum to be seen not as something imposed on the child by an alien group of teachers or administrators, but as a kind of public declaration of children's rights. This is much more in keeping with ideas of social justice in education. We should see a certain kind of knowledge and experience in science, mathematics, history and in politics and economics, etc., not as so much knowledge which is going to be imposed on children by teachers whether they like it or not, but as a kind of experience which is everyone's right to have access to. But without some kind of national declaration of why education is compulsory and why certain kinds of knowledge are given a high priority, discussions about equality in education are meaningless.

Schools will certainly need to work out detailed plans for this kind of curriculum, but it is also important to make certain other aspects of such a curriculum clear. A common curriculum need not be a levelling down, nor need it establish uniformity in education. There is a considerable difference between laying down basic minima which ought to be available to all children and stating standards above which children need not bother. No one is prevented from being an excellent driver by the very modest display of skills and knowledge required by the present driving test. I am not of course suggesting that education is anything like as easy as that, but it is a useful analogy to some extent. Merely laying down minimum curriculum requirements to be offered by the school does not inhibit in any way the high levels of achievement which will be possible for individual pupils.

Social justice in education does not mean equality in the sense of giving all children the same education. But it does mean that all children should have the right to real education, not an inferior kind of instruction and socialization. It will not be possible to achieve this kind of social justice without being more specific about a common core curriculum. Social justice in education must mean that all normal children have access to worthwhile knowledge and experiences.

REFERENCES

Addison, P. (1975) *The Road to 1945: British Politics and the 2nd World War.* Jonathan Cape.

Auld, R. (1976) *William Tyndale Junior and Infant Schools Public Enquiry.* ILEA.

Ausubel, D. P. (1968) *Educational Psychology: A Cognitive View,* Holt, Rinehart and Winston.

Banks, O. (1955) *Parity and Prestige in English Secondary Education.* RKP.

Bantock, G. H. (1969) 'Discovery Methods', in Cox, C. B. and Dyson, A. E. (eds) *The Crisis in Education.* Critical Quarterly Society.

Barker, R. (1972) *Education and Politics.* Oxford University Press.

Bell, C. (1928) *Civilization.* Penguin.

Benn, C. and Simon, B. (1970) *Half Way There.* McGraw-Hill.

Bernstein, E. (1968) Summarised in Hemmings.

Board of Education (1938) *Report of Consultative Committee on Secondary Education with special reference to Grammar Schools and Technical High Schools* (Spens Report). HMSO.

—, (1926) *Report of the Consultative Committee on the Education of the Adolescent* (Hadow Report). HMSO.

—, (1943) *Report of SSEC on Curriculum and Examinations in Secondary Schools* (Norwood Report). HMSO.

Bottomore, T. B. (1964) *Elites and Society.* Watts.

Bottomore, T. B. and Rubel, M. (eds) (1963) *Karl Marx: Selected Writings in Sociology and Social Philosophy.* Penguin.

Boyd, D. (1973) *Elites and Their Education.* NFER.

Burstall, C. (1968) *French from Eight.* NFER.

Burston, W. H. (1969) *James Mill on Education.* Cambridge University Press.

Burt, C. L. (1943) 'The Education of the Young Adolescent: Psychological Implications of the Norwood Report', *British Journal Educational Psychology,* 13: 126-40.

Clarendon Report (1864) HMSO.

Clarke, F. (1943) *Education and Social Change.* The Sheldon Press.

Cole, M. (1954) *What is a Comprehensive School?* London Labour Party.

Crosland, A. (1956) *The Future of Socialism.* Cape.

Dent, H. C. (1949) *Secondary Education for All.* RKP.

Department of Education and Science (1967) *Report of CACE (England): Children and their Primary Schools* (Plowden Report). HMSO.

Dewey, J. (1916) *Democracy and Education.* Macmillan.

Dworkin, M. S. (1959) *Dewey on Education.* Columbia University Press.

Eliot, T. S. (1948) *Notes Towards the Definition of Culture.* Faber.

Ellis, T. et al (1976) *William Tyndale, The Teacher's Story.* Writers and Readers Publishing Co-operative, London.

Engels, F. (1844) *The Conditions of the Working Classes in England in 1844* (Trans. W. O. Henderson and W. H. Challoner). Blackwell, 1971.

Entwistle, H. (1976) 'Working Class Education and the Notion of Cultural Adequacy', in *Cambridge Journal of Education,* 6, no. 3.

Evans, A. A. (1972) Quoted in Stewart, W. A. C. (1972) *Progressives and Radicals in English Education 1790-1970.* Macmillan.

Fabian Society (1901) *The Education Muddle and the Way Out.* Fabian Society.

Flude, M. and Ahier, J. (1974) *Educability, Schools and Ideology.* Croom Helm.

Ford, J. (1969) *Social Class and the Comprehensive School.* RKP.

Freire, P. (1970) *Pedagogy of the Oppressed.* Penguin.

Goodman, P. (1962) *Compulsory Miseducation.* Penguin.

Gray, J. and Moshinsky, P. (1938) 'Ability and Opportunity in English Education', in Hogben, L. *Political Arithmetic.* Allen & Unwin.

Gretton, J. and Jackson, M. (1976) 'William Tyndale, Collapse of a School — or a System', *Times Educational Supplement.*

Halsey, A. H. (1972) *Educational Priority,* Vol. 1. HMSO.

——, (1976) 'Is a Society Liberated or Repressed by its Educational System?', *Times Higher Education Supplement,* 22 October.

Halsey, A. H. and Gardner, L. (1953) 'Selection for Secondary Education and Achievement in Four Grammar Schools', *British Journal of Sociology,* March.

Hamilton, H. A. (1952) 'The Religious Roots of Froebel's Philosophy', in Lawrence, E. (ed) *Friedrich Frobel and English Education.* RKP.

Hargreaves, D. H. (1967) *Social Relations in a Secondary School.* RKP.

——, (1974) 'De-schoolers and New Romantics', in Flude, M. and Ahier, J. (eds) *Educability, Schools and Ideology.* Croom Helm.

Heafford, M. R. (1967) *Pestalozzi.* Methuen.

Hemmings, R. (1972) *Fifty Years of Freedom.* Allen & Unwin.

Henry, J. (1971) *Essays on Education.* Penguin.

Himmelweit, H. (1954) 'Social Status and Secondary Education since the 1944 Act', in Glass, D. V. (ed.) *Social Mobility in Britain.* RKP.

Holly, D. (1971) *Society, Schools and Humanity.* MacGibbon & Kee.

Holt, J. (1964) *How Children Fail.* Penguin.

——, (1972) *Freedom and Beyond.* Penguin.

Hooper, R. (ed) (1971) *The Curriculum.* Oliver & Boyd.

Illich, I. (1971) *Deschooling Society.* Calder and Boyars.

——, (1974) *After Deschooling What?* Writers and Readers Co-operative (London).

Jackson, B. (1968) *Working Class Community.* RKP.

Jackson, B. and Marsden, D. (1962) *Education and the Working Class.* RKP.

Jackson, P. (1972) 'An American View of De-schooling', *Forum,* 14, no. 3.

Jenkins, R. (1959) *The Labour Case.* Penguin.

Jensen, A. R. (1969) 'How Much Can We Boost IQ and Scholastic Achievement?', in *Environment, Heredity and Intelligence.* Harvard Educational Review Reprint.

Keddie, N. (1973) *Tinker, Tailor . . . . The Myth of Cultural Deprivation.* Penguin.

Labour Party (1918) *Labour and the New Social Order.* Labour Party.

——, (1934) *Labour and Education.* Labour Party.

——, (1945) *Let Us Face the Future.* Labour Party.

——, (1956) *Towards Equality.* Labour Party.

——, (1958) *Learning to Live.* Labour Party.

Lawson, J. and Silver, H. (1973) *A Social History of Education in England.* Methuen.

Lawton, D. (1973) *Social Change, Educational Theory and Curriculum Planning.* Hodder.

——, (1975) *Class, Culture and the Curriculum.* RKP.

Lowndes, G. A. N. (1937) *The Silent Social Revolution.* Oxford University Press.

Mandeville, B. (1723) *Essays on Charity and Charity Schools.* Quoted in Sturt, M.

Mannheim, K. (1950) *Freedom, Power and Democratic Planning.* RKP.

Marburger, C. L. (1963) 'Considerations for Educational Planning', in Passow, A. H. (ed) *Education in Depressed Areas.* Teachers College, N.Y.

Marsden, D. (1971) *Politicians, Equality and Comprehensives.* Fabian Society.

Mays, J. B. (1962) *Education and the Urban Child.* Liverpool University Press.

Mill, J., see Burston, W. H.

Ministry of Education (1945) *The Organisation of Secondary Education.* HMSO.

——, (1945) *The Nation's Schools.* HMSO.

——, (1947) *The New Secondary Education.* HMSO.

——, (1960) Report of a Committee Appointed by SSEC on *Secondary School Examinations Other than GCE* (Beloe Report). HMSO.

Moore, T. W. (1974) *Educational Theory: An Introduction.* RKP.

National Association of Labour Teachers (1930) *Education – A Policy.* NALT.

Neill, A. S. (1926) *The Problem Child.* Jenkins.

——, (1932) *The Problem Parent.* Jenkins.

Newcastle Report (1861) Report of the Commissioners appointed to inquire into *The State of Popular Education in England.* HMSO.

Parkinson, M. (1970) *The Labour Party and the Organisation of Secondary Education 1918-1965.* RKP.

Pedley, R. (1969) *The Comprehensive School.* Penguin.

Pelto, P. J. (1965) *The Study of Anthropology.* C. E. Merrill (Columbus, Ohio).

Peters, R. S. (1966) *Ethics and Education.* Allen & Unwin.

Pidgeon, D. (1970) *Expectation and Pupil Performance.* NFER.

Popper, K. (1945) *The Open Society and Its Enemies.* RKP.

Postman, N. and Weingartner (1971) *Teaching as a Subversive Activity.* Penguin.

Pring, R. (1972) 'Knowledge Out of Control', in *Education for Teaching* (Autumn).

Reimer, E. (1971) *School is Dead.* Penguin.

Rosenthal, R. and Jacobson, L. (1968) *Pygmalion in the Classroom.* Holt, Rinehart (New York).

Rousseau, J. J. (1911) *Emile.* Everyman edn.

Russell, B. (1916) *Principles of Social Reconstruction.* Allen & Unwin.

—-, (1926) *On Education.* Allen & Unwin.

—-, (1968) *Autobiography,* Vol. II. Allen & Unwin.

Sampson, A. (1971) *The New Anatomy of Britain.* Hodder.

Schools Council (1975) *The Whole Curriculum 13-16* (WP 53) Evans Methuen.

Shipman, M. (1969) 'Curriculum for Inequality', in Hooper, R. *The Curriculum* (1971). Oliver & Boyd.

Silver, H. (ed.) (1973) Equal Opportunity in Education. Methuen.

Simon, B. (1960) *History of Education 1780-1870.* Laurence & Wishart.

—-, (1971) *Intelligence, Psychology & Education.* Lawrence & Wishart.

Stanley, J. C. (1949) 'The Role of Instruction, Discovery and Revision in Early Learning', *Elementary School Journal,* 49: 455-58.

Sturt, M. (1967) *The Education of the People.* RKP.

Swift, D. F. (1965) 'Meritocratic and Social Class Selection at Age 11', *Education Review,* VIII, no. 1: 65-73.

Taunton Report (1868) *Report of the Schools Enquiry Commission* (Taunton Commission). HMSO.

Tawney, R. H. (ed.) (1922) *Secondary Education for All.* Allen & Unwin.

——, (1931) *Equality.* (Paperback edn. 1964). Allen & Unwin.

Thompson, G. (1921) *Newcastle Daily Journal,* 27 November, quoted in Vernon, P. E. (1957).

Trow, M. (1968) 'Research and the Racial Revolution in American Education'. Paper read at 16th Congress of the International Association of Applied Psychology.

Vernon, P. E. (ed.) (1957) *Secondary School Selection.* British Psychology Soc. Methuen.

——, (1969) *Intelligence and Cultural Environment.* Methuen.

White, J. (1968) 'Instruction in Obedience', *New Society,* 2 May: 292.

——, (1975) 'The End of a Compulsory Curriculum', in *The Curriculum* (Doris Lee Lectures). *Studies in Education. (New Series) 2.* University of London Institute of Education.

Williams, R. (1958) *Culture and Society.* Penguin.

Woodward, E. L. (1954) *The Age of Reform 1815-1870.* Oxford University Press.

Worsley, T. C. (1941) *The End of the Old School Tie.* Secker & Warburg, quoted by Boyd.

Yates, A. (1966) *Grouping in Education.* Wiley (N.Y.).

Young, M. (1958) *The Rise of the Meritocracy.* Penguin.

Young, M. F. D. (ed.) (1971) *Knowledge and Control.* Collier-Macmillan.

INDEX

DENIS LAWTON is Professor of Education and Head of the Curriculum Studies Department at the University of London Institute of Education. Formerly a teacher of English and history, in recent years he has been particularly concerned with the problem of planning the secondary school curriculum as a whole in terms of a selection from the culture of society. In this field his publications include *Social Change, Educational Theory and Curriculum Planning* (ULP 1973) and *Class, Culture and the Curriculum* (RKP 1975).

NOTES

NOTES

NOTES